.. wait, *WHAT?*

AKA,
"MOSSMAN'S LAW"

ELLY MOSSMAN

For written permission write to: Elly Mossman, bemossman@gmail.com

www.grampawasanalien.com

Editor: Teresa Schapansky

The characters in this book are real, as are the events. Some names have been changed to avoid embarrassment. It's not you.

Published by

Tough Old BroaD
PUBLISHING
Duncan, BC, V9L 0B4

2nd edition – revised

ISBN: 978-1-990414-27-5 – Hard cover

         978-1-990414-48-0 – Paperback

         978-1-990414-26-8 – E-pub

To Bill, the Love of my life.

TABLE OF CONTENTS   PAGE

INTRO

Weird things happen to us. More so than to a lot of other people I know. Maybe they just don't tell me, but I'm doubtful. Before I met Bill, I lived a pretty sedate life, which I always thought was normal. Then my life merged with the man I married, and suddenly ... stuff just seems to happen. Weird stuff. Things that make me go .. what was *that?*

I've learned to be somewhat wary in my day to day comings and goings. Some people would call it paranoia. I call it "being realistic". If I think there's a chance of 'It' happening, it will. Murphy's Law.

All the stories in this book are true, but the cartoons may be a little exaggerated - just so you don't think my world is really looney-tunes crazy.

I still say it's my husband's fault to begin with. Nothing much happened to me, at least not on the level of the incidents in this book - until I met him!

Move aside, Murphy.

..wait, *WHAT?*

ELLY MOSSMAN

Tough Old Broad
PUBLISHING
Duncan, BC, V9L 0B4

Oh Honey! You shouldn't have! And you want me to teach you how to use it, right? *

* see page 13, "DON'T APPLAUD, JUST THROW POOP"

PROLOGUE - THE FUN BEGINS

1991

I should have heard the warning bells at the beginning of my new relationship. Bill had gone to Nova Scotia for a month. The trip east to visit family for Christmas had been planned long before we met, and it meant that our first Christmas and New Year would not be spent together.

I lived in British Columbia's capital, Victoria at the time, on Vancouver Island, and I had promised Bill that while he was gone, I would drive to Sooke, a town west of Victoria to periodically empty his postal box.

My sister had come for a short visit. The two of us decided to take the opportunity to do some sightseeing, and get Bill's mail while we were out.

I had driven through Sooke once before, on my way to Port Renfrew, so I thought I knew the way. We chatted as I drove, and at some point I realized that things had suddenly taken on an unfamiliar look. My sister was no help, since she lived off-island and didn't know the Greater Victoria area at all.

The more I drove the more confused I became. For a while I followed roads that look vaguely familiar, all the while trying to keep what I thought was a westerly heading. In my gut I was starting to wonder if something was seriously wrong with what I thought I knew. But really, there was only one main road going to Sooke. You couldn't go wrong! Could you?

I had not seen any signs pointing the way to our destination, but still I drove stubbornly on, secure in the knowledge that there was only one road in, and one road out out of the place, and eventually I'd get there! At last we saw signs ahead. Dumbfound-ed, I read,

"WELCOME TO BRENTWOOD BAY".

I had driven east the entire way, instead of west! Hey! I never claimed to have a good sense of direction. But I'm proud to say I was now a full fledge member of that very exclusive club directly influenced by "Mossman's Law".

Rule #1: *If you're going somewhere, assume
you'll end up somewhere else.*

..? That's funny ..

What?

WATCH OUT
WE MOVE
BIG TRUCKING

I saw a truck come up behind me .. and now he's gone!

A HUNTING WE WILL GO
(The Gold Standard for Mossman's Law)

In the eighties, Bill lived in Nova Scotia, and he commuted by car each year to the BC coast, to fish for the four or five months the commercial season was open, starting and ending his trips in Prince Rupert. Each year, on the way home at the end of the season, he would make a layover in Edmonton, Alberta, at friend Bob's house.

He arrived as usual one evening, and during the course of the conversation, Bob asked if Bill would be interested in making a short hunting trip, along with his neighbour, Larry. The plan was to hook up with a group of guys, about an hour north of Edmonton. Bill was in, and they arranged to leave early the next morning in order to meet the others there at 7 AM.

Bill's car was loaded down with gear, dirty clothes and various items taken off the fish boat, that he needed to store at home, so his car wasn't available. Bob's car was practically out of gas and it was too late to find an open gas station the night before. By default Larry's car was chosen to travel in.

The next morning at 5:30 AM, the three of them piled into the car in gleeful anticipation of bagging themselves a nice batch of ducks. Winter meat. It all sounded good.

They were just outside of Edmonton, right in front of the Fort Saskatchewan Federal Prison, when a tire blew. Larry climbed out of the car and prepared to throw on the spare stored in the trunk. Unfortunately it was also flat.

The other two had no choice but to hitchhike back to Edmonton to get gas for Bob's car, and drive it to where Larry waited. The plan was then to take the flat with them, leaving Larry's car at the side of the road until the trip was finished. The tire could be fixed at a service station after the hunt was over, then continue home with both cars.

It was now 6:00 AM. Bob and Bill stuck their thumbs out and tried to flag down a passing motorist. Nobody stopped. Too late they realized, trying to hitch a ride in front of a Federal Prison was a tricky proposition. Finally at 7 AM a car stopped. The driver looked a little nervous and, after telling the man where they wanted to go and why, they rode in silence.

Bob, evidently, could stand the silence no longer. Intent on mayhem, he spoke up, asking Bill, "*Do you have the gun?*"

The car swerved a bit. Bill looked at Bob incredulously. "*What?*" Bob repeated the question, "*Do you have the gun?*"

"*Don't pay any attention to him!*" Bill tried to reassure the driver, "*He's just goofing off!*"

The man was noticeably perspiring now. "*W-w-where did you s-say you wanted to go?*" Bob gave him his address. They

Look at that! It must be duck hunting season again!.

4

arrived in record time, the doors still swinging open as the driver sped away, tires squealing.

Bill couldn't believe his friend. *"What the hell did you say that for?"*

"I dunno. Made the trip interesting."

Bob's car had just enough gas to make it to a service station where they filled up and headed back to Larry. It was now 8:15 AM. Larry was waiting patiently in front of the prison. The spare was tossed hurriedly into the trunk of the parked vehicle, and the flat likewise into Bob's trunk. All of them piled into Bob's car, and off they went to the rendezvous. The rendezvous had long disbanded.

Since they were there anyway, and, in spite of the setbacks, the three of them decided to do a little hunting on their own. Why waste the trip? By 9 AM they were positioned in a cold, boggy marsh waiting for the prize to fly over.

Quack, quack, quack, quack! Ducks! BLAM!! BLAM!!

OK, one duck, but a good shot that landed in the marsh with a splash. Bob was elected to go get it. Hopping from one dry hummock to another, he managed to get near enough to reach it. Barely.

As he strained to get hold of a feather or two, his foot slipped off the hummock and in he went. But he had the duck, and held it, triumphant over his head as he waded back. "Got it!!

Upon closer inspection the duck turned out to be a small one, but better than nothing. A few more would up the poundage count nicely.

It was the last duck that ever flew over their heads that morning. One o'clock came and went. Finally, Bill announced that he'd had enough, he wanted lunch, and he definitely had to get back on the road.

Cold, wet in Bob's case, and hungry, they piled back into the car and, with the duck, headed to the nearby town. A hot lunch and a few beers sounded good.

They dropped the flat off at a service station for repairs on the way. Bob, his mind on beer and lunch, opened the trunk, hauled out the tire, closed the trunk and rolled said tire into a service bay. Then he got back in the car and reached for the ignition … no keys. They'd been locked in the trunk. That hot lunch seemed farther away than ever.

"You don't happen to have a spare key do you?" Larry asked hopefully.

"My wife's got it."

"Call her!"

"She's not home."

But Bob was full of bright ideas. He removed the back seat, climbed into the trunk, thereby retrieving the keys.

Earlier that day they'd spotted an old pub on the way into town. They decided it would make a good spot for lunch. It looked a little worse for wear but those were usually the kind of places that served good hearty meals. By 3 PM the three weary hunters of ducks finally sat down to what they came for. A hot meal. Beer.

Bob settled into the booth and sighed gratefully. Off came the coat and the bootlaces untied, leaving his sore toes wiggling happily.

Finally, near 4 PM, sated and refreshed, they decided it was time to pick up the repaired tire, deal with Larry's stranded car and head home. Bill was getting anxious to be on his way east to Nova Scotia. The tab was paid and the trio pushed through the swinging doors and down the wooden steps to the street. Bob was the last one through the door and, as it swung shut, one of his still-untied bootlaces caught in the door sill. His foot jerked back abruptly as the top half of his body flew forward.

By the time Larry and Bill turned to see what the commotion was, Bob was already hanging, posed in a very awkward downward dog on the stairs with his face in the dust.

They were back in Edmonton at 5 PM. History does not tell us who got to keep the duck.

Rule # 2 - *If you have certain expectations, you can expect triple of what you didn't.*

PART I
LIFE WITH FISHERMAN BILL

GREEN IS THE COLOUR

Bill was a commercial fisherman on both east and west coasts of Canada for the majority of his working career. As a young man, he'd owned his own gas station, and then gone around the world on a research vessel owned by Columbia University, as a chief oiler, which gave him his taste for sea life. After that he'd worked as a longliner, dragger, and lobsterman, but at the time I met him, he was a BC commercial fisherman with his own troller, catching salmon off the north west coast of British Columbia.

He'd given me a few photographs taken a few years earlier when his oldest daughter Jill first fished with him, and I'd shown these to my parents long before they actually met him. My dad, being an avid sports fisherman himself, was instantly smitten.

We decided I would work as his deckhand. Both of us had gone through divorces, leaving neither of us much to start over with, and working as his deckhand would pool the resources. That, and I didn't want to be separated from Honey for three to four months at a time.

Sunshine, fresh sea air. It all sounded good. I think I gave the term "green" a whole new meaning. I'm not talking about that eco-friendly term either.

When I crossed the Hecate Strait for the very first time in 1992, on our way to the Queen Charlotte Islands (since then, they have been re-named with the traditional First Nations name of Haida Gwaii) the water was an impossibly calm, watery glass table. It was almost eerie. Clueless me, I thought this would be a piece of cake, never giving Mossman's Law a second thought. Life was grand!

We reached the Charlottes and made a stop in Skidegate. A cable had come off its block at the top of the mast, and tangled with another wire attached to one of the trolling poles. The low tide allowed the pole to be lowered down to Bill standing on the wharf, so the wire could be untangled, while my job was to climb the mast to the top, and hook the cable back over the block.

I took a hard look at the itsy-bitsy footholds on the mast that led to the block. But, this was all part of deck-handing, so gamely, up I went. From the deck it didn't look that high, but from the top, to which I now fanatically clung, I was very far removed from solid ground. Down on the wharf Bill looked ant-sized. However, I had a job to do, so I got to it.

I grasped the wire, heaved with all my might, and was in the process of slipping it over the block, just as the wake from the passing Skidegate Ferry set the *Blue Eagle* to jumping like a rodeo bull. The lowered pole did some crazy bounces on the dock and Bill danced back, letting go of the wire. I wrapped both arms around that cold aluminum and hung on, one foot firmly in the flimsy foothold, the other flapping free in the air.

When the swells died down I spent a few minutes persuading myself to stay up on the mast and get the wire properly in place. I got praise and compliments from Bill when the job was done, thereby passing my first test as deckhand.

We proceeded through the narrow Skidegate Channel that separated the two large islands that comprise Haida Gwaii, to the fog-enshrouded west side of Hippa Island, just in time for *THE OPENING*, (referred to in this manner, because each and every commercial fisherman holds this event as their own version of Mecca).

Bill had still not managed to fix either the sounder or steering mechanism at their secondary locations in the rear cockpit, before we left home. So, being primary deckhand, I was assigned to the wheelhouse to watch the inside sounder, and steer the boat, while Bill stood in the cockpit at the stern, to haul lines and bring in the fish. His instructions were, *"Steer around the shallow spots and stay on the tack."* ... um .. Shallow spots?

. . *SIGH*. .

'WORK WITH CELEBRITIES' THEY SAID. 'RUB ELBOWS WITH THE RICH AND FAMOUS' THEY SAID!

STAR
ROBERT REDFORD

SOME OF THE JOBS I'VE HAD AREN'T WHAT THEY'RE CRACKED UP TO BE!

Although I didn't know it yet, this was not enough info. I wasn't even completely sure what the term "tack" meant. I also didn't know what the bottom of that particular spot of ocean actually looked like. There are hundreds of massive pinnacles in the waters off Hippa Island that rise sharply to within a few feet of the surface and then fall, equally sharply to hundreds of feet deep. Think many pointy church steeples submerged underwater. Mossman said nothing about pinnacles. It would have helped. Maybe. Then again, maybe ignorance is bliss.

Dutifully, I kept an eye on the sounder's image .. and

watched the bottom rise steeply on the screen. I turned the wheel ... but ... which way? ... left? ... nope, the bottom still rose! ... I turned right! .. oops, now there was a boat in my way! .. and the bottom was still rising! ... steeply! I started screaming.

"BIIILLLL!!"
"Turn in, turn in!" Bill hollered at me from the stern.
"What??"
Never mind tack, this was a term I had never heard before.

I turned the wheel to the left again, but apparently not "in". Bill's voice reached an octave higher. **"Turn IN!!!!"**

I turned to the right. The bottom dropped out of sight. Aha! "Turn in" means turn right! Got it!

A few minutes later the bottom rose again on the sounder. I heard the instruction from the stern, "Turn out!!"

THE CATCH ON THE 'PICK-UP' IS BIGGER EACH TIME.
-IT'S A MATTER OF "GROW & TELL"!-
WHY, BRUCE FOUGHT FOR <u>HOURS</u> WITH A LUNKER FOUND FLOATING, HALF DROWNED, ON A BIG BED OF KELP!

HOW MANY FISH DID YOU SAY YOU HAD ??

OH MANY A STORY IS TOLD BY THE BEST, OVER GLASSES OF RUM AND ALE, ABOUT ALL THE GREAT TRIPLE-HEADERS THEY'VE HAD, OR THE ONES THAT CAME HOOKED BY THE TAIL!

AND MARK IS HI-LINING, WHILE EVERYONE'S PINING, FOR EVEN ONE FISH FOR THE DAY! BUT THE BIGGEST AND BEST OF THE FISHERMEN'S CATCH, ARE THE ONES THAT, **BY GOSH**, GET AWAY!

YOU'LL NEVER HEAR FISHERMEN TALK MUCH ABOUT THEIR LOST SNAPPER, OR DOGFISH, OR FLOUNDER. BUT, JUST YESTERDAY LEO LOST A BIG TUNA THAT WAS <u>CLOSE</u> TO A SEVENTY POUNDER!

YOU MAY JUST HAVE HEARD OF THE COOK WHO LOST DINNER, WHILE FILLETING COD FOR THE STOVE. SEEMS THE FISH TOOK EXCEPTION TO BEING THUS STRIPPED, AND TOOK OFF WITH NO MEAT ON HIS BONES!

WHILE BILL CRIES THE BLUES, WHEN A FLASHER IS NEWS ON THE END OF A **MONSTROUS** TAIL! YES, THE BIGGEST AND BEST OF THE FISHERMEN'S CATCH ARE THE ONES THAT, <u>BY GOSH</u>, GET AWAY!

"WHAT??"

... wait a minute ... if *turn in* means steer right, it stands to reason that *turn out* means steer left! Right? So my educated guess had me turning left.

Bill's voice went up another octave. "TURNOUT!! TUUURNNNOOUUUT!!!" Spit flew. My theory was shot to hell.

This went on for a while, me thoroughly confused, and yarding any which way on the wheel until, fed up, I abandoned my post and, in my boots and oilskins galumphed back to the stern. Matching Bill's octave and decibel, I screamed at him, *"I DON'T KNOW WHAT THE **HELL** TURN IN AND TURN OUT **MEANS!!!***

The darling man, in all his accumulated wisdom, had never bothered to fully explain these fisherman's terms which, had I known, would have been so much easier on my poor, frayed nerves. "Turn in" simply meant turn towards the nearest shoreline, and "Turn out" meant turn towards open water. Well why didn't he just say so?!

14

Things got complicated even further. I had the job of cooking meals in the galley, with the floor pitching wildly underneath me. Watching the sounder and steering around and around on the tack, in the middle of the cooking chore was still expected. The fishing stops for nothing. The spaghetti I made for lunch that day was topped with Parmesan cheese, the smell of which promptly drove me outside, to lean gasping over the rail.

My ignorance made that first day became my own personal day from hell. Bill hollered at me. The heaving rollers made me queasy enough to kill any pleasant thoughts I may have harboured in anticipation of this lovely experience. Those pinnacles evoked screaming headlines in my head. 'WOODEN BOAT SPLINTERS ON ROCKS! TRAGIC END!' I'm not sure if the term "multi-tasking" had been coined at that time, but I certainly learned what it meant.

Rule #3 - *If the kitchen floor moves, you may not be at home.*

RABBITS' FEET WON'T BE ENOUGH

One day, quite by accident, while preparing lunch in the galley, I opened a can of Pacific Evaporated Milk upside down. You'd think the world had come to an end.

Without warning, Bill, staring at the can in my hands, suddenly had a crazed look in his eyes. I'd never seen that before. He ordered me to fire the can overboard immediately! I again posed my most frequently asked question, "What?" The can was almost full, and my axiom, 'Waste not, want not', was enshrined into my DNA. His eyes went a little wild, and I thought for a moment that I would be the one to go overboard.

I learned very quickly that a can opened upside down on a boat - according to him - was extremely unlucky. So, into the Pacific that can of Pacific went! However, the next time I opened a can upside down, I ripped the label off so Bill wouldn't notice that he'd be having a spate of bad luck in the near future. I'm a rational person, after all.

Rule #4 - Rabbits' feet don't work. Lying
through your teeth does.

DON'T APPLAUD, JUST THROW POOP

The biggest positive impression I left with Bill was my ability to handle anything that stank. Big, strong, he-man Bill has a weak stomach. Specifically, anything that really stinks - really, really stinks, means he'll automatically gag like a cat with a giant hairball, and an undigested dinner sitting in the way.

And so it was that, early one morning I awoke and heard an awful racket coming from the head. In my sleepy stupor it didn't dawn on me immediately, that what I was hearing, was Bill retching. Then, after coming fully awake, and recognizing it, I wondered, *why?* He's not the sea-sick type .. and it was calm anyway.

I got up to see what the commotion was about. There was Bill, frustrated, with a wrench on the outflow pipe leading from the toilet bowl through the hull, retching as he worked!

"What are you doing?" I asked. In between gags, he managed to tell me he was trying to undo the pipe because it was plugged, and the toilet was backed up. I listened to him dry-heaving for a few more minutes and then ordered him out of the head. I took the wrench and managed to unscrew the pipe, remove the stinking mess, re-fasten the thing and get the water flowing again.

I think that impressed him enough to keep me on as deck-hand, in spite of my green-horn status.

The screaming continued over my inability to fully compre-hend the world of commercial fishing, and I discovered another, totally different side of the man I thought I knew. But on the plus side, I was never thrown overboard, or left on the nearest rock pile either!

That Bill and I were still together by the end of the '92 fishing season, speaks volumes for the relationship.

Rule # 5 - *When it looks bad, it might be good, maybe not. Ya takes yer chances.*

FALLING ON MY HALIBUTCHEEKS

I decided to follow Mossman into his halibut fishing endeavours. I thought I worked hard during salmon season but compared to halibut longlining, working on a troller was a Sunday picnic. My mind doesn't quite want to remember anymore. The memories have become a confused, nebulous fog, but I will try and describe it as best I can.

※ ※ ※ ※ ※ ※ ※ ※ ※

Bill became part owner of the boat he normally skippered for a good friend, Loman Daury. When tragedy struck and Loman died unexpectedly, Bill partnered with another skipper friend, to buy the old Prince Rupert longliner, *Zapora* from his widow.

The *Zapora* was a haywire boat. Everything was wrong with her, but like the Grande Dame she was, she seemed to plug along with baling wire and a wad of chewing gum. That's not the way Bill rolled however, and before the boat was taken out again, she was overhauled from stem to stern. There was no end to the problems, but finally the work was done. Or so we thought.

More than one "shake-down" trip was made, trying to rid the old girl of her deficiencies. On one of those fishing trips, we asked if Bob, another fisherman friend wanted to come with us to help.

"*No, not really!*" said Bob, wise man that he was. He knew the *Zapora* all too well and was legitimately leery. Finally, against

18

his better judgment, Bob allowed himself to be suckered in, such were Mossman's powers of persuasion.

To this day he still shakes his head over that decision, but the die was cast. We were three feet away from the dock when we discovered the first glitch. The reverse in the steering wouldn't engage. I still hear Bob in my head, saying in his usual dry tone, *This does not bode well!*

That entire trip was filled with blown seals, busted gaskets, gears that refused to work, oil that spewed and engine parts rolling in the bilge. I'm still not sure how we caught any cod, but we did. Poor Bob was giddy when he finally crawled off the *Zapora* onto dry land.

He still talks about it when prodded to do so, but like me, he is unable to remember details clearly. Like me, he just doesn't want to. Bob got lucky. He never had to go back out on the *Zapora* again. I did.

See Rule # 2

TAKE THIS JOB AND …

Finally, after endless hours and a lot of money, the old *Zapora* worked the way Bill wanted her to work, within reason. Then it was halibut season, which occurred between November and March.

One of the first trips was made in February, when the snow flew horizontally across the deck. We used octopus to bait the hooks, bought in solid, frozen blocks from a commercial supply place in Port Hardy. It needed to be cut into chunks for baiting.

By the time the first dozen or so were chopped up, in spite of wearing gloves and liners, my fingers were as frozen as those poor octopi. With those same frozen fingers, I then had to bait the large circle hooks, which would later be attached at intervals, with a 30" lead, called a gangion, and snap, to the 2 mile length of long-line. This setup made the complete string that would be played out behind the boat to lie on the ocean floor, enticing the halibut to bite. Snapping the baited hooks and gangions onto the long-line as it rolled off the drum and into the water from the stern, was also one of my jobs.

Of all of the work I had to do, the easiest, and simultaneously the hardest, was baiting those hooks while the gear was being hauled back in, bringing the fish on board. This was the real work, what we were out there for - catching those halibut. The line was brought in over the side, the gangion unsnapped from the mainline, the hook taken out of the fish's mouth, the gangion then thrown over to me, standing over on the other side of the hatch, ready to re-bait and coil back into a tub for the next set.

It doesn't sound that hard, does it? An experienced baiter could snatch the gangions being thrown at them, bait and coil with speed, and keep up. Unfortunately, I was not experienced. The hooks and gangions kept piling up in front of me, until I was slowed down even further because of the ensuing snarls! The inevitability of Bill starting to holler at me to speed up was ... well ... inevitable!

I was frustrated. And getting angrier by the minute. Other deckhands made it look so easy.

Eventually, after repeated heated bellows and commands from my captain to speed up, my temper boiled over. I dropped the bait in my hand, picked up the snarled mess in front of me, and prepared to heave the entire lot over the side of the boat. I caught Bill's eye.

"Don't you dare!" He says. For a moment we stared at each other. I don't know what he was thinking, but I was livid, and ready, in a fit of pure rage, to do something quite uncharacteristic for me .. then my common sense kicked back in. I remembered I was supposed to be in love with this man, and I really didn't want to throw his gear over the side, so I dropped it back on the hatch, and continued to work as best I could.

Later, when both of us had calmed down, we hashed it out. Bill realized, I was not as experienced as other deckhands, and he really did expect a little too much from me. I promised to try and work as fast as I could. I never did get as speedy as those other guys, but damned if they could look as good in oilskins as I could.

.. Everybody's gotta play One-up-man-ship ..

PHOBIA, WHAT PHOBIA?

For a few trips, we had a Newfoundlander on board as another deckhand. I couldn't understand a word he said, but we had fun with him. I found out he had certain phobias. Spiders. Women.

On the first trip out, Bill had him convinced that on our stop in Rose Harbour, we would be taking him to the dance, and setting him up with a nice girl. (In reality there is absolutely nothing in Rose Harbour, let alone a dance) He spent the next twenty four hours locked in his bunk because "all women had AIDS!".

During my turn at wheel watch one night I'd promised the Newfie I'd make him a fresh pot of coffee before he'd come to relieve me. He was appreciative. I made the coffee, but I had more in store for him than fresh brew.

After my little practical joke was set up, I was relieved of wheel watch by the Newfie. I lay in my bunk, situated off the passage near the galley, awake and listening as he made that quick trip to the galley for his first cup of coffee.

I'd purposely left the galley dark, so he had to feel his way to the cook stove. There was a crash of pots and a blood-curdling screech. He'd run smack into the mess of plastic spiders I had suspended on strings from the ceiling. Dozens of them. He thought he was a dead man. I'm going to hell for that one.

Newfie also had a thing about his hair, which was quite long and stringy. As far as I understood it, he'd been growing his hair to sell for big bucks to the wig making industry. I kept teasing him about the length, and telling him I would be cutting it right after I had cut Bill's. This was true in part. I cut Bill's hair regularly.

Newfie would harass me right back, all in fun, of course, to the point where I finally picked up a pair of kitchen shears and chased him off the deck, through the galley and up into the wheelhouse. He cowered in the corner screaming like a little girl, while I grabbed a small lock of his hair, snipped it off and scotch-taped it to the galley's cooler door. There it stayed for the duration, and every time he hassled me, I would point slowly and deliberately, from him to the lock of hair. That shut him up.

Rule #6 - If you plan on having an Achilles heel, footwear won't help. Get full-body armour.

DON'T MESS WITH THE COOK!

As well as baiting hooks and setting gear out, I also had the job of cook on the *Zapora*. There is a saying on a boat, *"Don't mess with the cook."* The implication being; You never know what they'll feed you!

After one trying, tease-fest too many between myself and the Newfoundlander, I decided to lay down my ace. I pointed my finger at him and said, *"You better not be hungry for the next few days! I'll be getting even!"*

At the next meal, I served everyone else the same thing. However, Newfie was given a plate of food that looked entirely different. That did it. Newfie, in a bout of unparalleled paranoia, refused to eat anything I gave him, even when I traded my plate of food for his. He was convinced I had messed with his meal.

I finally felt sorry for him, because he worked so hard, and every working man deserves to eat. Unfortunately, no matter what I said or did, I could not persuade him that it was all a practical joke.

Rule #7 - *Sanity is good. Paranoia is more fun.*

THE LOVER OCTOPUS

On their respective trollers, Bill had me as deckhand, and Leo had Michelle, female as well. The four of us went out to catch the *Zap's* halibut quota.

Bait was normally bought frozen in Port Hardy, and we went through a lot as the fishing season wore on. So, anytime we caught octopi on the gear, we had bonus bait. Free. Unfrozen. No cold fingers.

Here's the thing about catching octopi. If they aren't immediately hooked with a gaff, and kept away from the hull when the line is hauled in, they always manage to suck onto the outside of the hull, walk their way down to the keel and drop off, and the opportunity for free bait is lost.

Michelle was bent over the rail, gaff in hand, the minute Bill called "*Octopus!*" She wanted that fresh bait. She too was tired of frozen fingers. She managed to flip that eight-legged critter onto the deck, but she miscalculated the length of those suckered arms. In an instant, one of them reached out wildly, and had her right by the crotch!

I was in the galley cooking, and knew nothing of all this. I did however, hear the screaming. "*EEEEEEEeeeeeeeeeee!!!! GET IT OFF ME, GET IT OFF!!!! EEEEEEEEEEEEEEEEEEEE!!!!!!!*"

By the time I stuck my head out the galley door to see what was going on, she was in full flailing mode. The rubber gear she wore had no bearing on it. From that point on, anytime we caught an octopus, Michelle would stand well away from those thrashing legs. Tough deckhand or not, she was still a girl!

Rule #8 - *You'll find love in strange places.*
Proceed at your own risk.

CROWBARS AND AN OIL CHANGE

Zapora continued to be a cantankerous old lady. She was, after all, almost seventy years old by that time. One night we had to limp into Shearwater, with Leo sitting in the lazarette, a crowbar stuck in the rudder stock to steer. The steering mechanism had snapped.   Shearwater sounded like an interesting place. It was not.   They also didn't have the parts needed for the steering, but we managed to get it fixed by flying in the part needed. A day or so later we were back out on open water.

In all of our Zapora adventures, there is one unforgettable moment is permanently seared into my brain. Bill had to replenish the hydraulic oil tank during a wild, stormy night, but the tank was inexplicably located halfway up the inside of the hollow, aluminum mast. No one knew why such an awkward place was chosen, but there it was, and too costly to change around. Then the thing Bill hoped would never happen, happened.

A leak had developed somewhere, so, to prevent the hydraulics from running dry, the tank had to be re-filled. Bill struggled up the footholds in the mast, hanging on with one hand, the jug of hydraulic oil in the other. I sort of knew what that was like. Masts are masts.

It blew about 30 knots that night and most of the oil that Bill attempted to pour into the tank, ended up sprayed back over the deck, the railings, stanchions, the drum, and all the way back to the baiting claim, as Bill tried to feed it in. It was so slick it was impossible to walk upright on deck. We spent most of the next day crawling on our knees, slipping, sliding, and scrubbing every-thing down with degreaser.

Rule #9 - Common sense is relative.

APRIL FOOL

While Loman owned the *Zapora*, he lived, and kept the boat at the Comox, BC fisheries marina, so, because Bill served as skipper, it seemed expedient for us to live there too. When Bill bought the *Zapora* from Loman's widow the reason to live in Courtenay was moot. We began looking for a home closer to civilization.

We found a house in Chemainus, right next door to the parents of Bill's sister-in-law. We were visiting them one day, and noticed the cute little house for sale next door. We put in an offer immediately, and our mobile home in Courtenay found a new owner. Everything was going as planned.

Bill and I were scheduled to leave on a halibut trip, and we made sure all the papers were signed at the lawyer's. Bill gave him temporary power of attorney to finalize the sale of the Courtenay house, and put all our worldly belongings into storage. With all t's crossed and i's dotted, believing that everything was properly in place, we took off on the *Zap* for the top end of the Charlottes (Haida Gwaii).

On April the first, as Michelle and I were setting out gear off Langara, Bill came out to the stern and pronounced solemnly, "*I just got a message via the Coast Guard. The sale of the house in Courtenay fell through!*"

I am impervious to April Fool jokes, having been on the receiving end of a few too many from Bill. "*Yeah, right!*" I said back at him. I kept setting gear. Bill insisted, "*I'm not joking, it fell through! The guy never showed up to sign the final papers!*"

"*Sure, sure!*"

He went back into the wheelhouse. Leo looked after him. "*I don't think he's kidding.*" he said to me. I stared at Michelle, who stood across from me at her station. She shrugged. "*It's April first. Who knows?*"

We finished setting that string, and I confronted Bill on the bridge. "*You were kidding, right? It's April first and this is one of your jokes! Tell me this is one of your jokes!*" But there was no mistaking or denying the meaning of that stare.

So there we were, out in the middle of the Pacific, and not able to do a thing about it. We moved to Chemainus anyway, and put the mobile home back on the market, renting it out until it sold two years later. In the meantime we were subjected to a motley parade of renters who proceeded to trash the place.

Rule #10 - *When in doubt, refer to Rule #2*

My memory still conjures up a brew of circular hooks and snarled gangions, slimy yet frozen bait, wild storms, humongous halibut, dragging anchors, snapped lines, a roller coaster stern, an inundation of cold green Pacific water, and a makeshift replacement gasket involving my embroidery scissors and a piece of thin felt. I was never so glad as when I got back to the sedate business of trolling for salmon.

The old *Zapora* is still a working boat. She is now geared up with freezers, painted a menacing black, and fishes offshore tuna. At around 100 years old she can still be seen in the off-season, at her berth at the Fishermen's Wharf in Victoria, BC.

PART II
THE MORE THINGS CHANGE, THE MORE THEY STAY THE SAME

DOES THIS STILL COUNT AS FISHING?

At a certain point we could see the writing on the wall. Commercial fishing had become a rich man's game for the most part, and salmon wasn't paying very well. Expenses were sky-high and the take-home money was negligible, so Bill sold the licence and later, the Blue Eagle, having already divested himself of the Zapora the year before.

There is nothing worse than Mossman bored. He needed to work, and began looking for a job. I could have given him one, but he wouldn't look good in an apron, and it didn't pay well.

The opportunity of a boat transportation business came Bill's way, and, once he got his Class 1 licence it seemed to be a perfect fit.

The Road to Hell is paved with good intentions ... and also a few presumptions. The business produced more stress in the twelve years under his command, than the previous twenty five in the fishing sector. I had to peel him off the ceiling more than once after dragging himself home from a long day of work. I don't think he slept at all the first year.

He once elicited more than a few stares from motorists as he trailered a boat through Ladysmith, one hand on the wheel and the other holding a very bloody rag to his badly bruised nose because he'd taken a header on a dock.

On a certain day, I found a police cruiser in my driveway. The officer had a bundle of papers in one hand and Bill's briefcase in the other. *"Does a William Mossman live here?"* This is not a reassuring question coming from a cop at your door. Unwanted images entered unbidden into my head. The fear factor rose just a titch in my gut, but I needn't have worried. Mossman was doing Mossman.

It seems that a load of paperwork, along with a briefcase were found on the road just above us. Bill had left the stuff on the back deck of the truck, and driven off. I walked up the road with the officer, to see if there was anything else, and found his cell phone and more papers in the ditch.

Back it up between those trees, around the corner, under the overhang, and into the carport ... oh, and don't run over the flowerbeds!

Bill was forced to slow down considerably, when he fully dislocated his shoulder, falling over the trailer as he caught his foot in a strap. You'd think he'd be used to his equipment by now.

IF AT FIRST YOU DON'T SUCCEED ...

Bill only knew two speeds; full speed ahead and stop. With both of us working odd hours, we sometimes didn't see each other except in passing. I'd see him going in the opposite direction in his big yellow diesel being chased by what looked like a very large bathtub toy. Honk. Wave. Hi. 'Bye! This, folks, was why we started taking vacations.

In 1999 we planned our first long overdue, honest to goodness holiday. The coming January, 2000 we would spend a week and some in Nova Scotia in the snow, which I would tolerate, and a week in the sun in Cuba, which I would tolerate a lot more.

I desperately tried to lose some weight so that the Cubans wouldn't die laughing when they saw me in a bathing suit. In retrospect they probably would have died anyway, laughing at Bill's lily-white legs. In his adult years, Bill had never worn shorts, and his legs defied the description of 'white'. It would have been better had we both kept our long pants on, each for our own reasons, but the shorts were on, Cubans or no Cubans.

We were lured to Nova Scotia that year with tales of balmy weather and sunny skies by certain individuals who shall remain nameless. In anticipation, we stepped off the plane in Halifax, only to be stopped dead in our tracks, frozen on the spot to the tarmac.

During that first week we were assaulted with two blizzards, so it was with no great difficulty that I boarded an Air Transat flight from Halifax for sunny Cuba. Helllooooo sunshine! Trust me, the following was because of us.

The thermometer in Cuba read an unusual 18 degrees Celsius, 10 degrees colder than normal. This did not feel especially cold for us northerners, but it was certainly well below normal for Cubans, as evidenced by the locals, who went around shivering, and wearing woollen mitts and hats. We traipsed around in shorts, t-shirts and mild denial.

Bill bought a pair of shorts for the first time since his childhood, especially for the occasion, but his legs never lost their lily-whiteness. Come to think of it, I thought I heard a little Cuban snickering once or twice.

WHAT MAKES YOU THINK THE LUGGAGE WAS MIXED UP?

I really don't know what the Cubans thought of us. I'm sure the little "mojito girl", who sold us drinks in the resort lobby every night, only saw dollar signs. They may dislike Americans, but they love those American dollars. She was crazier than our Newfie from the Zapora, climbing into Bill's lap trying to sell him a drink. She knew three English words, "drink", "yes" and mojito. Now that

I think about it, *mojito* is a Spanish word, so she really only knew two. I don't think she understood what the word "no" meant, because everyone in the lobby ended up with a drink or two in their hands. I ended up with a hankering for *mojitos*.

Rule #12 - *If it's cold where it shouldn't be, you can blame us.*

...TRY..

I'm still convinced the cold temperature was our doing, because the following January we decided to drive to San Felipe, Mexico. Our friends had always regaled us with stories of sunshine and warmth in January without fail, to the point where we just *had* to go. We were starving for sunshine and warmth in January, and this was a sure thing. So we went.

Got us a nice little condo just off the beach. It took three heaters to keep the place lukewarm, one of which was in the bathroom so we could shower without turning into popsicles.

I never changed out of my winter clothes. After four days we looked at each other and decided that if we were going to be bundled in winter coats, we might as well go where we had an excuse. The Grand Canyon is spectacular - and cold - that time of year.

Rule #13 - *Beware of friends who tell you about "sure things".*

35

...TRY AGAIN

On our third trip a year later, we seriously wondered if the jinx would finally be broken. A friend had persuaded Bill, we should try Thailand. Once you go there, he said, you never want to go anywhere else. Obviously, he didn't know Bill very well.

Much to our relief, we knew whatever curse had been put upon us by some angry Cuban god, in a fit of offended sensibilities over Bill's lily-white pegs, had finally lifted! It was so hot I couldn't walk five minutes without leaving puddles in my wake, but I didn't DARE complain! I knew if I did, I'd be punished with death by a thousand sand-flea bites ... which we both ended up with anyway, so *somebody* must have complained. It was still the best vacation I ever had, hands down. I cried when we returned to snow on the ground in BC.

Rule #14 - *Never complain about anything. The opposite of what you don't like is just as bad.*

ENCOUNTERS OF THE WATERY KIND

We usually planned our January vacations well in advance the preceding year, but one year, because of the weather, and a few other unmentionable factors, they sort of went up in smoke. No loss. Bill wanted to drive down to the Gulf of Mexico, although I still, to this day can't understand why anyone who drove 150,000 kilometres a year would want to do a driving vacation.

There was much hemming, hawing and feet dragging about the logistics of it all. Finally it was settled. I went to sleep that night in driving mode and when I woke up, I was flying! This particular phenomenon is called, "Mossman Style". I discovered that I was destined for Ixtapa, Mexico on a one week, all-inclusive package, arranged while I lay snoozing in my nice warm bed earlier that morning.

Two days into the vacation, I was revelling in the sun, sand, and balmy temperatures, cavorting in the surf, feeling as if I never wanted to go home again. Then, inexplicably two feet in front of me was a curling-over wall of water. I had a nano-second to get the impression of the parting of the Red Sea. I also used that nano-second to brace myself ...

I came to, bumping along the bottom of the ocean on my tush, with my bathing suit down around my ankles. I had enough presence of mind to know I was only in waist-deep water and that I'd look a little foolish standing up. I managed to retrieve my suit just before it followed my mask and snorkel into liquid oblivion. After hauling the straps back up over my shoulders, I stood up. It felt suspiciously heavy, like I had raked half the beach into my suit. But what felt even more strange was my face, my arms, my chest, my back. Had I somehow been hit by a Mexican bus? What was it doing in the water anyway?

Bill was a little closer to the shore and had been swamped by the same beast. I floundered around in the water trying to feel for the snorkel gear underfoot. Since the surf had roiled the sand up, I couldn't see anything in the water. When I hollered at

It must be a new kind of plant life!

Bill that I had lost my mask, my mouth felt like I had been to the dentist. What was a dentist doing in the water? Was he Mexican? Was he in cahoots with the Mexican bus driver? My arms and hands tingled and my upper body reverberated from the bus hit.

I saw Bill, and then a half dozen other people, looking at me funny. I just wanted my mask and snorkel back, and considered doing a cross-section search.

"Never mind your mask, look at your face!" Bill yelled.

I wasn't sure what all the excitement was about. But, I dutifully let one of the resort attendants drape a towel over my shoulders and march me to the resort clinic, where, as instructed by my husband, I looked at my face in a mirror.

Two inches had been added to the width of my head, and my mouth was pushed to one side like Popeye. At that moment, I realized I would have the mother of all shiners. My face had played contact sport with the bottom of the ocean.

Now I had two choices; (1) Pretend nothing's amiss, or (2) Spend the rest of our vacation with a bag over my head.

I opted for choice one. For the rest of the week, with my face almost entirely black and blue, we toured Zihuatenejo, went para-sailing, and took a sunset cruise, entered - and won - a pole dancing contest (I come by it naturally - don't ask) and went shopping at the local markets. I got asked how I was feeling in at least four different languages.

Our waiter, a big Mexican by the name of José, was shocked, and stared at Bill like he'd done it! I had to convince him he didn't. José acted like my bodyguard at mealtimes for the rest of our stay. I came home with a very special "Ixtapa Tan".

Rule # 15 - *You really do come back from a vacation looking different.*

Rule #16 - *Not all tans turn out the same colour .*

Rule #17 - *It takes an amazingly long time for sand to finally exit your ears*

THE JOYS OF 'GETTING AWAY'

Part III

CONFUSION ON THE HOME FRONT

I didn't bother with a level. I got a good eye for this kind of stuff.

MONEY TO BURN

The question, *"Have you seen my wallet?"* is an oft-asked question in our household. My usual answer; *"Check all your pockets."* This time, however, the thought of his pants already loaded into the washing machine flitted across my mind as I said it. You all know the scenario: Stop the washing machine; fish out the pants; feel the pockets; extract soggy wallet.

Bill was understandably upset, although I failed to see the reason why. I maintained it was his job to check his pockets before throwing it in the laundry, and he maintained it was mine before throwing it in the washer. *"How am I going to use this money? I was going out to pay some bills! I can't give them wet money!!"*

"Why not? It's freshly laundered!" I thought, with tongue in cheek, although I never said so out loud, Mossman's suddenly not-so-cheery mood, you understand. ... and here's where the brainwave kicked in.

"No problem," I thought, *"I'll just dry the bills real quick in the microwave."* So I did just that. No more than 7 seconds after popping a fifty and two twenties into the microwave, it began producing flashing and crackling, mini grenade explosions! I ripped open the nuker door and pulled out the bills, each with a smoking

42

strip down one side. They were neatly scorched with a row of little black holes. Oops! Forgot about the metallic security strips.

If you thought Bill was perturbed before, now he was incoherent when he saw his ninety bucks half burnt! *"No worries,"* said I, out loud, *"the bank will replace these, no problemo!"*

I needed to run some errands anyway, so I took the burned and still wet bills with me. There really was no problemo exchanging the bills, but, as I walked out of the bank I could still hear the tellers laughing. Well I'm glad I was able to make somebody's day a little cheery.

Proud of myself that I has remedied the situation, and come home with crisp, new and dry bills, I walked into the house, fully prepared to wave these crisp, new and dry bills under my husband's nose and say, "See? All's well that ends well." I never got to say it.

"Mossman's Law" was not done with us yet. The look on Bill's face should have told me something was up, but I could only stare at him dumbly, as he greeted me with, *"Well, I've done it now!"*

Only then did I notice a small, brown, shrivelled and unrecognizable piece of something between his thumb and index finger. *"I tried to dry it out in the oven, and look what it did!"* It was his leather wallet.

Well... aren't we a pair.

Rule #18 - *Not everything you put into an oven produces something edible.*

SECRET INGREDIENT

It was Christmas time, and the dinner was being held at son, Owen's house. To lessen the burden of cooking for Angie, since she was large with child that year, we did pot-luck. I arrived with the fixings for a large spinach salad and dessert.

I hate to admit it, but I have a certain number of vanities that I indulge in. One of them is my nails. I have short, stumpy fingers, and my nails don't grow well. So, I used stick-on nails for special occasions. This was one of those occasions.

So here we are, Angie and I in the kitchen, busily prepping all this delicious food and engaging in a wonderfully bonding conversation. I had finished putting together a very large layered trifle, complete with fresh fruit and fake rum, and had almost completed the spinach salad. As I was rinsing my hands so I could chop the egg for a garnish, I suddenly found myself staring in horror at my fingers.

I must have made some sort of sound, I really don't remember, but Angie asked in alarm, *"What's the matter?"*

I could barely utter the words. *"My nail is gone!"*

"What?"

"My nail is gone!" I held up my left thumb as punctuation.

We stared at each other in shock and then, as one, down into the salad between us. We knew what we had to do. Angie brought out another bowl and both of us dug into the salad, transferring it little by little into the clean bowl, inspecting each piece carefully. No nail.

When the entire bowl had been examined, it was clear to both of us that there was only one place left to look. The trifle.

My beautiful trifle! The salad was one thing. You can't do much damage to a salad, but this concoction had been put together lovingly, carefully. It was a masterpiece. How could I take it apart, root through it, and not leave any evidence of the rooting?

Then I envisioned someone biting down on a plastic stick-on nail during the course of dinner. I envisioned my ex-husband, my fastidious ex-husband, or my equally fastidious son, biting down on a plastic stick-on nail.

The trifle came undone. The offending item never materialized. No stick-on nail ever surfaced anywhere in that kitchen. The trifle was rearranged and covered over with a forgiving layer of extra whipped cream. Angela was sworn to secrecy. I never wore stick-on nails again.

Rule #19- *Everything fastened, comes loose. Everything.*

HERE COME DA FUDGE!

Our third grandson was born in August of 2007, but by then I didn't have much time to get my grandmotherly butt over there. It was all the fault of the fudge. Fudge. Chocolates. Marshmallow fudge creations. Not to mention truffles.

One of our Kiwanis members had made the brilliant suggestion that a good way to raise money for our charitable work, would be to make and sell home-made fudge and chocolates. What a great idea, we thought. Kiwanis had never heard of "Mossman's Law"!

And so, I found myself totally immersed in chocolate. Along with two other ladies, I spent nine months making and selling the stuff. I was sick of chocolate! I swore if anyone gave me chocolates for Christmas that year, I'd scream.

When do I get a taste? Or, do I just lick you off?

If there's one thing I've learned, it's this: Never, NEVER try selling chocolate during the hot summer months at an outdoor farmer's market. No matter how much money you're raising, the trauma of melted chocolate breeds wicked little voices in our heads, I swear!

We are happily selling, when we hear someone say, just as a customer is buying chocolate .. *"Excuse me, but this chocolate is all bent out of shape!"* This is not good advertising for us, nor good PR.

The wicked little voice in my head is saying, *Easier to eat.*
Out loud I say, *"My apologies, I'll get you another one! Here you go, enjoy"*

"This one is soft too!"

46

Giggling, the wicked little voice says *My, my. We're picky, aren't we?*

Out loud, *"How about some fudge?"*

"I'd rather have chocolate."

Miffed, the wicked voice goes on, *Now we're just entitled!*

I drown out the wicked voice by being extra helpful. *"Let me look in the cooler ... here you go, nice hard chocolate. Again, enjoy!"*

Chagrined, the wicked little voice slinks away in disgust. Kindness rules for one more day. We are the Kiwanis!

A quick table inspection after this, reveals that most of the chocolate items are indeed, very soft. It becomes worrisome, as visions of unidentifiable brown puddles on the table, slide around in my head.

The chocolate is all placed carefully in the cooler to harden, and fresh hard chocolate items are put out. The procedure is repeated every fifteen minutes. Every weekend. All summer long. There's no satisfaction in baby-sitting melting chocolate.

Then there are the hours of cooking, shaping, pouring, smearing, wiping, licking, stirring and above all, smelling. I can personally guarantee that if you are a chocoholic, making chocolates, fudge and truffles for a straight nine months will cure you!

Oh yes, guess what my very first Christmas present was that year? You got it ... a box of chocolates! Regrettably, I was too polite to scream.

Rule #20 - Rule #5 applies, in reverse

THE ROAD TO RENO

In spite of all the hoopla that went into the structure of our respective days, Bill and I decided to take a quick, four day weekend away to Reno, just to relax. Our intention was to drive to Seattle first, and then fly from there at seven in the evening. It was cheaper than flying from Vancouver.

As we stepped out of the car in the Sea-Tac Airport parkade, Bill noticed a stream of suspicious looking liquid trickling out from under the car. He began to swear and popped the hood of the car. Sure enough, we had a blown radiator. The location of the car in the parkade did not facilitate a tow job, so we started the car and drove slowly out, keeping a wary eye on the temperature gauge.

A nerve-wracking ride to find a service station while watching that gauge climb is not conducive to the beginning of a relaxing weekend.

Finally, with no service station in sight, we were forced to stop when the needle hit red. We ended up in the parking lot of a seedy looking motel. While the hood was popped open and steam billowed out in great clouds, we conducted a frantic conversation with the motel desk clerk, who seemed a little oblivious to just how serious this was. The conversation that followed sounded like this:

"Hi! We're from out of town and we have a problem! Our radiator is broken, and we need to have the car towed to a service station, so it can be fixed. And our plane leaves in an hour!"

The desk clerk is looking at us with a vacant stare, as if we are speaking Martian. Finally, she says, "I don't know any towing companies."

This was before the internet came into wide-spread use, you understand, and I ask, "Do you have a phone book?" There is another blank stare, then, "Umm ... Yes?"

The girl seems to need prompts from us to speak. "Can we look at it?"

She slowly hands us the telephone book from under the counter as if it were the original Gutenberg Bible. I ask her, "What's your area code here? We don't want to call someone from too far away. We don't have a lot of time!"

She looks at us as if we are still speaking Martian. "What's an area code?"

There seems to be a critical need for specificity. "You know, the first three digits before your telephone number? To indicate the area you live in?"

The blank stare continues. "Uhhhhh ... I don't know?"

We decided at that point that it would probably be better if we looked up a Toyota dealership, and take the number with us to Reno. We could call from there. We hoped the dealer would arrange a tow and fix the rad, so, like spastic scribes we frantically jotted down the numbers, along with the name and address of the motel. Then we called a taxi to take us to the airport, where we would make our flight - if we were lucky.

We had no choice but to give the car keys to Ms. Blank Stare. Bill gave her a twenty with the promise that we would arrange to get the car out of her parking lot by the next day. She seemed to be happy with the twenty.

We barely made our flight, and made our calls to the dealership from the hotel room. The next morning it was more calls from Reno to Seattle, which took a good part of the day. We returned to Seattle a day early so we could get to the dealership while they were open. I played a total of a half hour that weekend, playing the slots. No winnings.

Oh, by the way, we had to pay extra to get the return flight changed. Then the drive home from Seattle to Vancouver just in time to catch the last ferry back to the Island.

Rule #21- *Use the terms "cheaper" & "relaxing" together at your peril.*

THINGS THAT GO BUMP IN THE NIGHT

Our cat, Whoopi began bringing dinner home after she learned how to use her new cat door. Her version of take-out. Sometimes she would try and teach me how to hunt and kill, when she'd bring home dinner live-on-the-hoof. I would have a critter

50

presented to me, still moving, and the cat would sit back and watch as I rounded up whatever it was she'd brought me. Sometimes it was a mouse, or a snake. Once, when I'd been especially good, I got a rat.

All three of us ended up enclosed in my tiny bedroom ensuite, Whoopi watching, me whacking, and the rat trying desperately to get out. The rat and I traded places at the door three times, while Whoopi sat on the toilet tank cleaning her feet. She was done with us.

One evening will live in infamy for a long time. Whoopi had yet again come home with take-out. A wee mouse. Still wiggling. Fresh in our minds was a recent mouse cadaver found stuck in the refrigerator motor, stinking up the kitchen with that delightful and distinctive smell. I did not want to ignore this mouse. Bad things happen when I do.

The scene in the living room was not our normal, cozy arrangement that evening. All furniture was piled in the middle of the room. Bill had the broom firmly gripped in hand, and I was relegated to the floor, cheek pressed into the carpeting, eyeball to eyeball with the mouse. I narrowly missed the wild swipe of the broom.

The mouse disappeared from one spot only to re-appear miraculously in another. Another whack with the broom and another near-miss for me. Bill swore there were two! Midnight came and went.

We devised barriers to corner the critter, hauling in pieces of lumber and bits of wall-board. The living room looked like a war zone.

Finally we caught it, and as I marched it out of the house by the tail, the little snot bit me! On a normal day I usually am quite kind to animals, but on that day, I took great delight in heaving it across the road into the ditch, my conscience clear.

Rule #22 - *If you want a quiet life, never have a cat door.*

DINNER CAUGHT ON THE HUNT TASTES SWEETER!

Part IV
RETIREMENT - ARE WE HAVING FUN YET?

SPECIAL DAYS ARE HARD TO FIND

Honey, the business was sold a month ago. Let go of the wheel and step away from the truck.

Finally, Mossman hung up his tie-down straps and retired. July 1st, Canada Day was approaching, and our boat converted fish boat-live-aboard, "NoHurry" was finally launched. It was the perfect opportunity to take to the water. We motored out to the middle of Ladysmith Harbour to watch the fireworks. We took friends, munchies and a case of brew.

Anchored in the bay, enjoying the last warm rays of sunshine, sipping a beer with a mouthful of chips was 'The Life'. It couldn't get any better! A few other boats had arrived and they too, seemed to be appreciative of the ambience. It got progressively darker. The fireworks probably wouldn't start until nine-thirty or ten; we were unclear as to the exact time. Didn't matter, we were enjoying ourselves immensely!

So we waited. It was now dark. We waited some more. Bill put the binoculars up and peered over at the shore. There didn't seem to be a lot of activity, and he thought it strange that it was so quiet. Beer in hand, we continued to wait patiently, but still no fireworks on the horizon.

Across from us, on the other side of the bay, we noticed a rowboat was in trouble, and considered pulling anchor to help. Before we could, another small craft came sidling up to them and helped them to shore. Not long after that a Coast Guard dinghy came putt-putting alongside us asking, *"There was a rowboat out here having a few problems. Have you seen it?"* We had, and informed the officer that we had observed another boat take the occupants to shore, so they should be OK. They waved in acknowledgment, and then asked us, *"Are you enjoying yourselves?"*

"Oh yes, it's a fine night out here! We just wish those fireworks would start!"

At that moment, our question of 'when' was answered, and I wondered how he could have kept a straight face as he told us, *"You'll be waiting a long time! They don't start until a month from now, on BC Day!"*

Rule #23 - Expectations are over-rated.
Closely related to Rule #2

55

THE TOILET GODS MUST BE ANGRY

The year after the *"NoHurry"* was launched, we managed to enjoy a lovely summer onboard. On our last trip of the season we took our friends, Lyle and Mary with us to Desolation Sound, along with our aging cat Whoopi (she of mice catching fame). Despite a few glitches, we had a great trip. These glitches included the power supply, a lost cat and a toilet.

We had two power systems on the boat, 12 volt and 110, with an inverter. Early on, the inverter decided not to work. Although after the fact, the fix was simple, Bill wasn't yet familiar enough with the workings of an inverter to know how to get it started again. So we did without anything electrical. No microwave, no percolator, no toaster. No George Forman grill. We boiled coffee on the old diesel burning, fish boat stove we'd kept on the boat. Ditto for the cooking. We also had a stainless steel BBQ and a Coleman stove. We weren't going to starve.

Our biggest concern was the computer chart program connected to the onboard GPS. With all the charts programmed into the computer we could see exactly where we were every step of the way. If we couldn't get the computer working, we'd have to cut the trip very short. However, a stop at Powell River let us buy a converter plug, the laptop was plugged into the twelve volt system and *Hot Damn*, we were good to go!

For almost two weeks we explored the coastline, went canoeing, fished for crab and prawns and soaked up the sun along with a few beers. Sound idyllic doesn't it? Ah, but there is a price to pay for all that hedonism. We were headed home when the price was extracted.

I had paid a visit to the head, installed with an electric marine toilet. It ran off the 12 volt system, so it worked fine, thank goodness. When I flushed that morning, I discovered it was not draining very well. I flushed again. Still not draining very well. A third flush. Not a good thing to do.

The toilet bowl began filling up faster than it would drain. I'd hoped against hope that I could flush the crap away enough so I wouldn't have to deal with it. Nope, the thing finally filled to the top of the bowl, and began spilling over very slightly. The toilet was hopelessly plugged!

My announcement that no one would be using the head anytime soon was not met with enthusiastic cheers. Bill said something unintelligible about my pile of something something. I didn't get into it, thinking the conversation would probably just go to crap anyway. (Well, it would!)

I opened the porthole and shut the door, making it off limits to all. I sort of hoped that the whole works would soften up enough to flush out later, but the toilet-gods weren't smiling.

An hour later I was faced with an irresistible voice in my head, demanding that I flush one more time, which I succumbed to, while the voice in my head screamed, *don't do it don't do it!* ... and then I was up to my big toes in you-know-what!

I wished for a plunger, not that it would have done any good. If you know the inner mechanisms of an electric toilet, you'd know a plunger wouldn't have done a thing. Someone had flushed something down, that should never have been flushed. Whatever it was, had gotten stuck in the mechanism, and everything built up around it until the inevitable hot mess.

We were almost into Deep Bay and decided to call Cliff, our wharfinger friend. Bill explained our situation. He, plunger in hand, met us as we tied up.   As we all know by now, the plunger wouldn't have solved anything, although the thought was appreciated.

We resorted to solution #2. Bill and Lyle began taking off the drain hose at the base of the toilet, but Bill was quick to leave when he began to retch uncontrollably as the hose-end began to ooze brown goo. As a matter of fact, he literally flew out of the cabin onto the deck. I did mention, didn't I, that my big, strong darling has no stomach whatsoever for stink? We resorted to solution #2. Bill and Lyle began taking off the drain hose at the base of the toilet, but Bill was quick to leave when he began to retch uncontrollably as the hose-end began to ooze brown goo. As a matter of fact, he literally flew out of the cabin onto the deck.

I brought toilet paper! Does that help?

I did mention, didn't I, that my big, strong darling has no stomach whatsoever for stink?

At that point Bill decided to get a plumber's snake (solution #3) so the two men left for local hardware store.   Cliff's wife, Val had come down with some ice-cold bottles of Caesars, and we sat on the dock drinking, waiting for the boys to come back. When they did I took over for Bill, helping Lyle work at the toilet. The snake was employed and, while Lyle sat on his knees, bent over with both hands on the hose, I stood off to his left, ready with a pail to catch any .. um …. stuff.

Suddenly, the hose let go with a resounding "POOMPH!!" Lyle sat, frozen on the spot, his entire face and upper body covered with foul smelling excrement. I couldn't help myself. I began to laugh. I think Lyle did too, from the way he was shaking, but he wisely kept his mouth shut.

We sent him, along with a change of clothes, to the showers. The entire head from about three feet down, was covered with a layer of poop. My bottle of bleach was going to be well-used, but first I needed a little more fortitude in the form of another caesar. Whatever was stuck in the hose was reamed away with the snake. Forever after, there was a sign posted in the head above the toilet, which read:

DO NOT FLUSH ANYTHING DOWN THIS TOILET, UNLESS YOU HAVE EATEN IT FIRST!

As soon as I haul this trap, we can eat!

Rule #24 - Never flush a third time.

I didn't think the only thing in the trap would be kelp!

Shut up and eat! Greens are good for you!

I *TOLD* you never to say, *'I'll swim to China before I eat greens!'*

59

And what about that lost cat? She decided to go wandering one day, which we didn't discover until we were almost set to leave. We'd tied up at a small dock at some remote village somewhere in the boonies, and were now set to untie and make our way to the next destination.

We searched for hours, looking, calling. No cat. I had visions of leaving her there to fend for herself, which set my heart palpitating. It felt like leaving a kid behind. It was almost dark, the dock lights had come on, and we were still standing on the planks discussing possibilities, when out of the corner of my eye I saw a small body with 2 gleaming eyes come sauntering down the length of the dock. Relief was spelled, T H E C A T C A M E B A C K. More grey hair followed.

I THOUGHT THE DESERT WAS DRY!

After retirement we followed the example of most retirees, and decided to head south for a few months during the winter. During one of our our snowbird sojourns in Lake Havesu City, we weathered a storm that blew in from California. There were flash flood and tornado warnings all throughout southwestern Arizona, especially in the Phoenix area, and tons of snow in Flagstaff.

We weathered our own version of a flash flood in our rented mobile home. The thing leaked! The kitchen, the bedroom, the bathroom, the hallway, rain came in everywhere. The note we found earlier in the medicine cabinet, which stated that *"if there is water in the light fixture, don't turn the light on"* should have told us something.

We stayed busy with every pot, bucket and pail we could scrounge up. The water came down the inside of the windows in sheets, so I rolled up bath towels and lined the window sills, especially in the bedroom. The bed was pulled out a foot from the wall so the pillows wouldn't get wet. I placed baking pans under the window, in a hopeless attempt to catch the water running down the inside of the wall.

The towels were wrung out, thrown in the dryer and fresh rolled up towels were stuffed in the sills to sop up the water. The dryer ran constantly for the good part of two days with this routine. It was almost reminiscent of being back on the boat, trying to keep ourselves from drifting away. This was definitely a fair-weather house.

To think, we left BC behind to get away from the rain and snow. We kept getting emails from home about now nice and sunny the weather was. I hoped against hope they were lying!

When our lease was up, they of the rental agency didn't even bother to compensate us for washing down the entire inside of the house, even if it was inadvertently. Nice.

Rule # 25 - *If it's raining inside, the "open umbrella = bad luck" rule doesn't count.*

WHERE ARE WE, POR FAVOR?

We decided to give San Felipe, Mexico, another go as a vacation destination. Surely to goodness the cold snap we previously experienced wouldn't happen again, would it? We didn't know it yet, but San Felipe had something much more delightful in store for us.

We needed to first connect with our friends, who were already there, seeing as they were the ones who had arranged our rental accommodations, and knew the location. The last time we visited them at home, Bill had gotten the directions to their RV site in San Felipe but, not only had he forgotten to bring it along, he'd totally forgotten he had them at all. Dalton again, gave street directions to Bill via Skype, a few days before we left Arizona.

Are you sure the travel agency didn't say any-thing about this?

I'm still not sure if it was Dalton's directions, or Bill not following them, but we drove around the bumpy streets of San Felipe far too long, driving around like dumb gringos, asking directions to the "Playa Linda RV Park, por favor", if we were lucky enough to find someone who spoke English. After about an hour, on our third time around the circuit, we noticed a familiar figure waving at us from behind a wrought iron gate. Dalton.

"Playa Linda" was not an RV park at all, but a private home and property, called "Playa Linda" by the owner. No wonder nobody knew what we were talking about.

Dalton took us down to the condo complex in the late afternoon. It was a small one, 8 units in all, and apart from the resident manager, we were the only occupants in the entire building. We unloaded the car, and got the key from a slightly bonkers, and very un-Mexican manager, a Gringa, who warrants a whole chapter all by herself, which follows next.

Rule #26 - Not everyone can give or take directions. In such a case, following your nose works just as well.

CONDO RENTAL - MEXICAN-STYLE

It was near dinner by the time we parked, recovered from our unwilling excursion through San Felipe, gone to inspect the condo, met the rather suspiciously odd American condo manager, and dropped off the luggage. Then, we all went out to dinner to a local hole-in-the-wall. After spending 20 winters in San Felipe, Dalton knew exactly where they all were. We had a bowl of *sopa* and a few *quesadillas*. Over *cervezas* we BS'd with some other friends of his, then said goodnight-see-you-tomorrow, and headed back to the condo, breathing a sigh of relief that things seems to be progressing normally for once. The temperature was just as we liked it - warm.

When we got back to the condo and unlocked the deadbolt, the door latch was firmly engaged, and no matter what we tried, it wouldn't open. The door had two locks, a deadbolt and a lock on the latch handle. Earlier, we'd discovered through trial and error, that the key was for the deadbolt. However, in our attempt to discern which lock this key opened, we had inadvertently turned the latch handle to the "lock" position. There was no way we could get in.

As we were pondering our plight, while having visions of sleeping on the beach, Tammy*, our American, alcohol-propelled manager came by. By this time she was fully loaded, and this was, in her mind at least, a major catastrophe. Luckily, we had cracked a window to air the place out a bit. The windows were held fast against break-ins by a stick jammed into the inside window channel, and we thought that if one of us could get our arm through, we could flip the stick out with something long, slide the window open and crawl through.

MOUSICAN HAT DANCE

The skinniest arms happened to belong to Tammy, a very drunk Tammy, I might add, so she was elected for this part of the operation. Meanwhile, I had found a piece of stiff wire and was trying to pick the lock. I can't pick locks, but I was desperate. Bill was on the hunt for anything that would give us a little better leverage in prying the stick out of the window channel.

An hour went by, and Tammy, not sobered up much, had worked herself into a wild-haired, red eyed, snot nosed, bawling state as she stood on the patio chair with her arm through the window. The broomstick she held almost looked as if it was working away of its own volition at the stuck window stick. I heard her howl something about the end of a rope and her miserable existence.

Jack*, an elderly friend of hers happened by, and he lent a much needed non-alcoholic perspective to the situation. Jack came armed with a wire coat hanger and Bill had found his ice scraper. While I tried to turn Tammy's howling down a notch, the two men got the slider window out of the bottom track, pried the two windows sections far enough apart with the ice scraper, inserted the coat hanger and got the butt end of the stick up and away from the glass. Then the stick was pushed away until it clattered to the floor. There was never a sweeter sound!

Tammy, calmed down by now, climbed through and unlocked the door from the inside. Duct tape was immediately placed over the now open lock knob to prevent any further such mishaps.

* names have been changed for obvious reasons

64

Rule #27 - When in Mexico, stick to Mexicans.
The Gringos are crazy.

THE UNDESIRABLES

I spent some time in a dentist's chair in Mexico during the winter in Havesu City. I'd already had some needed dental work done at home, but the cost was prohibitive, and I'd run out of serious money. Los Algodones, Mexico has some excellent dentists, most trained in the States. I suspect that Algodones was created especially for Gringos coming to Mexico for cheap dental work and eyeglasses.

It is the norm when going into Algodones, to leave your car in a huge parking lot on the US side of the border and walk across the line into Mexico. Nobody even looks sideways at you as you walk through the chain link gate. No border guard checks your passport, or stops you to ask what business you have in their fair country. Walking across is also easier than trying to find parking in the narrow congested streets. Coming back into the US, however, is a whole other kettle of fish. I will elaborate on that soon.

The following year we stayed in Yuma, Arizona, and my first appointment for the serious work was up. I'd arranged a mid-afternoon appointment because I'd learned the previous year that if you arrive in the morning, you end up getting accosted by the Mexican vendors, as you can stand in line for anywhere up to three hours, getting back through customs into the States. Thousands of people from all over the western States and Canada come to Algodones for dental work and eyeglasses, and of course the tourist circus is in full swing. Better that you're finished with everything in the late afternoon after the crowds have gone, so you can stand in line for only a short while.

Of course, there's always the option to sit on a barstool, sipping Margueritas for the rest of the day. On the surface that might seem like a good idea, but don't try coming back into the States while snockered. Those US border guards are not to be trifled with.

My second appointment two days later was also in the afternoon at 4 PM. Again, by the time I was done, the crowds were gone and I anticipated an easy walk through customs. By this time I felt like we were old hands at it. Perhaps this played into the situation I found myself in.

As I exited the dentist's chair, Bill said, *"We're in big trouble now!"* I was clueless. *"What do you mean?"* I could tell by the look on his face that something was seriously up, but for the life of me, I couldn't imagine what.

"We don't have our passports!" At first, my head addled with dentist stuff, I said, *"No, we have them. They're in the...."* ...and then I remembered where we were ... and where the car was. Silly us had left our passports in the console of the car on the US side of the border.

Feeling very foolish, we walked up to the first customs wicket available, and discovered that the border guards at Los Algodones are no friendlier than their cousins up at the Douglas border crossing in Washington State.

As we went up together to explain our situation, the Customs Officer stabbed his finger at Bill and barked, *"You! Get back in line!"* Bill slunk back to the front of the line. I was on my own. While I explained our predicament to Officer Surly, Bill had been waved over to the adjoining wicket where he explained his version of the whole sad story.

He must have a golden tongue or something, because the custom's officer let him through on his driver's licence as ID alone - after a lecture about passports.

I, on the other hand, after also showing my driver's licence, got escorted by my own personal, very burly, Officer Surly II to the detainee room. I couldn't produce proof of Canadian citizenship in the form of my passport, currently taking up residence in the car. On the other side of the US/Mexican border.

Bill stood waiting near the exit, not realizing that I would not be going anywhere for awhile. As I was led away I managed to hiss at him in passing, *"Go to car! Get passports! Go!"*

In the detainee room I was greeted by the sight of some very unhappy looking Mexicans seated on benches, and a young red-haired kid who, for some to-me-unknown reason, was showing the bottoms of his sock feet to an officer. His shoes were on the counter being watched over zealously by another. My driver's licence was now also in those zealous hands.

I sat between two Mexicans, while the nature of my crime was passed on. I got looks and eyebrows. I felt the need to explain, *"My husband has gone to the car to get my passport."*

No response, just more looks and eyebrows. Minutes ticked by. We hadn't parked that far from the border fence, so I knew Bill would be back any moment. The shift change came in, more looks and eyebrows my way, and the new guard, after examining my driver's licence for some time, (I could only surmise that our BC drivers' licenses were somehow fascinating material) finally leaned across the counter and asked me how come I didn't have my passport with me.

Once again I explained, *"I accidentally left it in the car on the other side of the border but my husband has gone to get it and he should be here any second!"* I began to wonder if they just wanted to hear me say it one more time because they couldn't believe anyone could actually be that stupid!

I waited some more. Still no Bill. The unhappy Mexicans were led away, one by one. The red-headed kid was marched out. I had visions of Guantanamo.

Finally the guard leaned back across the counter and told me he would release me, but never enter the US again without my passport. A telephone call to the outer customs area brought my burly Officer Surly II back, who escorted me outside, looking for Bill. I had more visions - the two of us going round and round the building, forever missing each other. We finally connected back inside customs, I waved my open passport at the officer in the detainee room, flashed a smile at burly Officer Surly II, and promptly vacated the premises.

Rule #28; If it's not stuck to your forehead,
you won't have it when you need it.

GETTING OLD MAY- OR MAY NOT - HAVE ITS PERKS

As my 65th birthday approached, someone must have taken note. One day I got a package in the mail, addressed to me personally. I had no idea who it was from.

It's always nice to get an unexpected parcel in your post. I've learned though, that if you want to hang onto those warm, fuzzy feelings at finding a present in the mail, never do what I did. I opened it. Inside this nice, unexpected parcel was a sample pair of Depends™.

I put the thing aside and concentrated on getting my cook back. Let me explain. Upon retirement, I gave Bill the new designation of 'Cook', thinking he'd be less underfoot if he had something to do. So now, while Bill was busy recuperating after his long-awaited knee replacement surgery, I was relegated once again to doing the cooking.

"ON SECOND THOUGHT, YOU PROBABLY DON'T NEED ANY!"

I was promised that cooking duties would be resumed by my resident chef in short order. I could hardly wait. In the meantime, I slaved over a hot stove, shuttling plates of food and glasses of water, or cola, or milk, along with other and sundry items back and forth between kitchen and dining table, bedroom or recliner.

A week after Bill got home, the shoulder surgeon's office called with a date for his shoulder repair. He'll be in the recliner recuperating again for a few months with his arm in a sling ... wait ... what?! ... Oh crap!!

By the time the shoulder surgery and second knee replacement was over and done with, I had a brand-new husband. I may need to have a few parts replaced myself just to keep up with him, (if I had to pick one, it would be my entire body) but all in all, I'm still in fair shape and wouldn't have it any other way ... except for the Depends™.

Rule #29 - Not all gifts contain good things. Open at your own risk.

****

Mossman's Law applies to our future generations, just as it did to past generations of Mossmans. I know this because Bill's father once went out to buy a fridge and came home with a stove. Similarly, our freezer packed it in a while back, so we went shopping for a new one and came home with a nice recliner. Mossman's Law.

Related to that is the Law of Proximity. If you're near us you'll feel the effects just like we do. Take the example of a lunch outing with our friends of the infamous toilet blowout on board "NoHurry". They should have known better by now.

****

THE ROAD TO NOWHERE

The Raynors pick us up at 11:30 AM and all I know is that one minute we are bumping along the old logging road towards Port

Renfrew, our destination within reach, hungry, looking forward to that salmon burger. I'd had only a piece of walnut bread that morning, and then KA-*BLOOEY!!!*

We are suddenly off the road after a teeth rattling bang, bump and lurch! An inspection reveals not one, but two flat tires. We have driven over a section of asphalt that had broken away, creating a very sharp edge. There is only one spare in the trunk. There is no cell service, so the cell phone that Bill forgot to take with him, wouldn't have been of help anyway.

It's raining and I am the only one who had the foresight to bring a waterproof coat. Bill's bald spot is getting wet, so he drapes a purple towel, fished out of the trunk, over his head.

The boys take the tires off and discover that the rims of both wheels are ruined. The rinky-dink donut spare is put on the

front and Bill, still with the purple towel on his head, flags down a pickup carrying a load of empty pop cans.

The guy is not in a friendly mood, with problems of his own, something about a broken rear end, not sure whether he's referring to his rear or the truck's. Maybe it's the purple towel. The pickup drives on. Us girls suggest it might be helpful if Bill winds the towel around his head, turban-style so he could at least pass himself off as a harmless religious type, before he stops the next car.

The next pickup is friendly, probably thanks to the towel, and offers to take them back to Cowichan Lake so they can phone BCAA. Thank goodness Lyle has remembered to renew his membership. Mary and I will stay with the car and await their return. Lunch looks very far away now.

Cars go by, ogling the two tires on display at front of the car. One stops, a young couple. Mary gets out to explain that the men have hitched a ride for help and that we are OK, but she adds, "We're a little hungry, though. We never got to Port Renfrew for lunch!"

The girl reaches into the back, produces two buttered slices of banana bread and offers this to us. The guy pulls up half a bag of tortilla chips. Looking around for more, the girl holds up a can of beer. What a nice young couple!

The couple drive on and we realize we have scored big-time! As we sit munching on the goodies, we contemplate what else we can mooch off of passing motorists ... if they stop. The possibilities are endless. Another car stops and it is my turn. "Yeah, the men have gone to Lake Cowichan for help and we're OK, just a little hungry. Never got to Port Renfrew for lunch!"

Unfortunately, this does not produce any food. Maybe it was the banana bread hanging from my mouth. The next car is Mary's turn, and she delivers the same lines. No food. We will have to make do with the existing menu. There is, unfortunately, no more beer on tap.

After a few hours contemplating which car, pickup, trailered boat or camper might have eats, what kind that might be, and how good it would taste, a very large flat-deck tow truck appears around the bend. The driver is greeted by us with, *"I hope you brought something to eat!"*

It is 6:00 PM when we, along with the wounded PT Cruiser are delivered back to Duncan. A sub sandwich and drinks have been thrust into our hands, which we eat in the tow truck. The washboard helps digest this fare on our return trip. It makes for a strange lunch, but Lyle is forgiven immediately, after he takes us out to dinner to make up for it.

The Raynors now believe that they are members of the Mossman's Law club.

Rule #30 - *When driving, always have four spares in the trunk.*

****

At this point I'll interject a few stories about the other members of this exclusive little club. As the offspring of Mossman, my three step-daughters are just as susceptible. They are Mossmans, and this law is therefore, hard-wired into their DNA.

JANA - HERE KITTY KITTY!

1982 - The knock came late one evening after the girls had been put to bed. A man stood on the doorstep. *"I`m sorry to* disturb you, but do you own a cat?" Bill answered yes, they did indeed own a cat. What colour was it? Gray. Oh dear.

The gentleman was very contrite. "I'm afraid I've just killed your cat! It just ran out in front of me! I couldn't help but hit it. I'm really sorry!"

Bill took the dead cat and put it in the garage for the time being. It was dark out, and he would bury it in the morning, after the girls had gone to school and daycare. The problem Bill and Judy had now, was how to tell their daughters about the cat's demise. The cat belonged to Bill's baby, four year-old Jana, and she was especially attached to Chimo. Hearing about its death would be traumatic, they thought.

Many times the next morning, Jana asked the question, "Where's Chimo?"

"He's gone out hunting!"

And again, "Where's Chimo? I want to play with Chimo!"

"He's out somewhere. You have to go to daycare now. You can play with Chimo when you come home."

After the girls had gone, Bill took the now-stiff cat corpse and buried it near the backyard fence. All day, Bill and Judy mulled over how they would break the news. They finally decided to lessen the loss, by having another kitten ready for her when the girls got home. They ended up with two. Another story.

Jana inspected the new additions very carefully, played with them for awhile, and then asked the dreaded question. "Where's Chimo?"

Bill decided to give her the raw truth. "Well, Chimo was killed by a car, so he can't play anymore."

"Where is he?"
"He's gone."
"Where?"
"He's just gone."
"But, where did he go?"

Stubborn like her father, she wouldn't leave it alone. She had no concept of "dead" and had to know where the cat was. Finally, Bill informed her that he had buried Chimo in the backyard.

"Can I see him?" Jana asked. This was not the question Bill expected, and at this point he thought it best to be brutally honest.

"Well, he's dead." Still she remained persistent.

"But, I want to see him."

There was no choice but to take her out to the backyard. He dug into the soil until he found the body, reached down, pulled the cat out by the tail and held it up. It was now wet, matted, dirt covered and stiff as a board. Jana stood there staring with large eyes fixated on her beloved pet. For a few awful seconds daddy didn't know what she would do.

Finally, she made the solemn pronouncement, slowly in her very own unique Nova Scotia twang, "Doesn't .. he .. look .. turrible!!"

Relieved that she, for one so young, was being rather pragmatic, Bill very carefully asked, "*Shall we put him back into the ground?*" Jana thought that would be a good idea. So the cat was buried for the second time that day. Jana tamped down the soil with her feet. "*Does that hurt him?*" she wanted to know.

Bill answered, with relief at her calm demeanour, "*No that doesn't hurt him. He can't feel anything anymore.*"

Satisfied, Jana returned to the house and her new kittens. The cat exhumation had met its objective.

D'ya think this is the right way to the mall?

Rule #31 - *Dead cats do have their purpose.*

JILL - WANNA GO FOR A DRIVE?

1989 - At the age of sixteen Jill had been instructed in the art of driving by her father. She also spent her summers fishing on the troller, delivering regularly to Prince Rupert, on the north coast of BC.

While in town, as newly mint-ed teen drivers are fond of doing, Jill wanted to get in as much behind-the-wheel time as she could. They'd been lent a car from a Prince Rupert friend so, with cousin Jamie, who was an extra visiting deckhand on this trip, she took the borrowed car on a short, four block trip. For "practice".

She agreed to let Jamie drive on the way back. He needed the "practice" too. Jamie executed the driving portion of this exercise beautifully, but the parking got the better of him.

The parking lot was situated at the edge of a 100 foot, boulder strewn embankment, that plunged straight down into the Prince Rupert Harbour. As Jamie eased the car into its parking spot, he got the gas and the brake mixed up, and shot the car right over embankment. The only thing that saved them from the water far below was a large boulder halfway down, that caught the front end of the car as it fell.

A tow truck was called, and a lot of explaining done to the owner/friend. Another member - maybe even two - had been initiated into the Mossman's law Club.

Rule #32 - *Good deeds never go unpunished. (This one may have been borrowed from somewhere, but it fits)*

JODI - WE'RE DOING THIS IF IT KILLS US!

2006 - A wedding was in the works for the first of Bill's girls to get married. Need I mention that weddings are already a breeding ground for 'things that go awry', without the added handicap of being a Mossman's Law Club Member?

Jodi and Chris had planned a wedding in San Diego, aboard a catamaran. Right from the get-go the flight out of Calgary did not go smoothly. They were supposed to leave Calgary at 7:00 AM on the day before the wedding, but their incoming flight had been prevented from landing by Calgary's fog. They would not make the connecting flight from Denver to San Diego, and instead were left standing at the airport with spring break's thousand other passengers. The airlines said, "go home". According to them, there would be no flights out for a long time.

In all this time, Jodi had been holding her long, white wedding dress on its hanger high over her head, so that it wouldn't trail on the floor, or get wrinkled in the suitcase. She and Chris began to make phone calls. Going home was not an option. They were getting married the next day. Hell would have to freeze over first, but call after call to various airlines resulted in nothing. It looked as if hell would be getting a little chilly.

At long last the fog lifted enough and two first class tickets were found for an exorbitant sum each, on a flight bound for Vancouver. From there the possibilities of getting to San Diego were bigger, even if it meant they had to drive. The pair finally arrived in Vancouver, Jodi still holding her wedding dress high in the air.

Daddy, I have the awful feeling I forgot something important!

After two stand-by tickets were in their hands, they discovered that the first flight out to San Francisco, where they could get a connecting flight to San Diego, had no seats left.

There was also the added burden of obtaining a marriage license from the State of California, in order to marry there, so they needed to be anywhere in California, in reach of a city hall before the end of business hours. Time was running short. They were told there was little chance of getting to San Francisco until after the close of the business day.

They made the next flight out and San Francisco was under their feet by 2:30 PM on the 24th. Just before three they were at the licensing counter at city hall, Jodi still valiantly holding her arm straight up above her head with her dress safely off the floor. It was already after business hours, but someone felt sorry for the bridal couple and processed the marriage license.

All I said was, "you sure you want to do this?"

Back to the airport then, and at 9:00 PM a flight deposited them in San Diego, nine hours late, only to discover that the luggage had not arrived with them. Chris' tux, Jodi's shoes and other essentials had gone truant. Only the dress, still held up high on its lofty perch at the end of Jodi's numb fingers, was in evidence.

The beings that govern Mossman's Law must have taken pity on the bride and groom. Much to everyone's relief, on the morning of the wedding, just before an emergency shopping trip, the luggage arrived.

Rule #33 - *Marry as close to home as possible. You never know if the wedding gods are having a bad day.*

SIGH!

..wish I could
do something
about these
thighs ...

BWAAWW

BBRRRRR

I'd go for liposuction if
I could afford it ...

..yup ..just
suck it out!

?

BWAAAAAA

BWAAOFFPHOOMP!

Dream on, Thunderthighs

RRRRR

Lloyd's place
was broken
into
last
night!

That's the third
time this month!
We need a dog!

BEWARE
OF
DOG

Ten bucks says she doesn't
make it to the front door!

80

Part V

DOWNSIZING DOESN'T MEAN LESS

THE TENANT

When Bill retired we had visions of extended winters away in warm places, and a lot of travelling to enjoy. But, we needed to divest ourselves of a home and property that required a lot of upkeep. Travelling and property upkeep do not blend well, so we decided to downsize.

As we were preparing to sell our Chemainus home of fifteen years, we realized that the ramshackle storage shed at the back of the property would have to come down. It provided housing for leftover, old commercial fishing gear and car parts. There were coils of halibut ground line, fenders, fish tote boxes, rolls of carpeting, underlay, and other odds and sods that Bill didn't know where else to put.

Oh yes, there was also a family of raccoons living in it. Bill had opened the double doors to begin the chore of emptying out the shed, when there was a racket next to his ear that sent him flying out of the shed. Momma raccoon had positioned herself inside a roll of carpeting that was propped up beside the front door. She'd climbed up the roll, stuck herself halfway out the top so that her head was level with his, barely a foot away, and screamed. He thought a banshee had been let loose.

Why didn't you tell me you leased for three months ...

... I can postpone the demolition you know!

She had babies inside, near the back, and if it was quiet we could hear them chittering. Every day we'd listen, waiting for when they'd be gone.

Neither of us had the heart to tear the place down around them. We were also scared to death of Momma.

Every day Bill tried hurrying the evacuation process along by pounding on the side of shed with a crowbar. One day there was no more chittering. I cautiously opened the door and stuck my head inside. Nothing. I stepped into the shed with my gloves on, ready to tackle the mess. Two steps in, I heard the most unholy sound beside my head that I ever wish to hear. I stumbled out of the shed with my arms wrapped around my head, fully expecting my ears to bleed. Momma hadn't moved her brood at all, and she wouldn't until she was good and ready.

It was another two months before we finally got an excited call from our neighbour to come and see. Here was Momma and three babies, little furballs rolling around outside the shed. We watched them waddle leisurely down the back drive, cross the road to the other side and wander off into the brush, without so much as a backward glance. The shed came down in record time before Momma had the chance to change her mind.

Rule #34 - Open shed doors slowly and carefully. Odds are there's something on the other side, that will scare the crap out of you.

JUST A WEE DRINKIE

One April, I went over for a day's visit to my second daughter-in-law. It was Kim's birthday and my plan was to treat her, son Dwight, and grandson Erik to lunch. Kim loved sushi so I took them to a sushi bar. The food was wonderful, but that was the end of the pleasant visit.

My jaw started to ache. By the time we got back home, I was in agony. An abscessed tooth had decided to rear its ugly head. This was before my Mexican dental work.

After repeated pill popping, which made no difference to the pain careening around in my mouth, Dwight suggested I try swilling with rum. Swilling?? If I'm going to put rum in my mouth, I'm going to swallow! He had just the ticket, a bottle of screech, which I began downing, after first swilling, of course. The pain didn't lessen, but I was removed from it by an arm's length.

We decided I should return to the island on an earlier ferry than planned because of my 'condition'. I shall not differentiate whether said 'condition' was the impacted tooth, or the inebriation. The two had inexorably become one and the same.

Dwight drove me back to the ferry terminal and, as I boarded the ferry back to the island, I held a brown paper bag tightly to my chest. Don't remember much of the two hour trip back, but I think I walked sufficiently straight as I left the ferry.

I'm only presuming that Bill picked me up, because I know I got home. That's about all I'm sure of. That, and the empty rum bottle.

Rule #35 - Rum fixes everything.

84

A CAT NAMED MOSSMAN

We discovered that Mossman pets are not immune to the *Law* either. A new kitty entered our lives shortly after we moved, after the demise of our beloved and cantankerous Whoopi. With new kitty in tow, we set sail - OK motor - on another boat trip. We wondered how she would take to this new adventure. She didn't seem to be afraid of anything, and we discovered all too soon that Bebe was a true Mossman.

One evening, as we lay at anchor, Bill and I were just finishing up the dishes, when there was a clatter out on deck. Bill's immediate reaction was, "OMG!! Bebe's gone overboard!"

Sure enough, the deck chair lay on its side leaning over the rail, and the cat was nowhere to be seen. I peered anxiously and disbelieving over the side. No cat, only a suspicious ripple on the water. I had visions of her sinking straight down to the bottom, but, still not quite believing that scenario, ran down to the lower deck to see if she was behind the back cabin and then peered into the cabin itself to look for her. Still no cat.

I looked over the rail again but saw nothing. I ran to the port side, my heart in my mouth, and there, paddling furiously around the stern was a bedraggled and angry looking little animal. She looked up at me as she passed by. If looks could kill I'd be dead now.

Bill and I both scrambled for the dip net and scooped her out of the water. After a good rub with a towel and some furious licking on her part she was as good as new but it took awhile for our hearts to stop racing.

We re-created what had happened from the position of the deck chair, and what we knew of her habits at home. She loved to jump up to the back of any chair and view her world from on high, and she had done the same thing with the deck chair, which promptly overturned out towards the rail due to the momentum and her weight, dumping her into the drink. I never saw her jump to the back of the deck chair again, but her curiosity stayed intact.

The skiff was usually stored, resting on its side on the swim grid. However, it was now in use, tied to the stern, and towed behind us. Bebe sat on the rail and watched it, and we knew she was itching to jump into it, to check the thing out.

At one point she had actually jumped down off the rail onto the swim grid, to try and get closer, but the skiff was not within jumping distance. I ordered her back into the boat. Unfortunately, her nails couldn't dig in as she made the jump back up to the rail. I heard a high-pitched 'skeeeeee' sound, as her claws, unable to hook into the fibreglass, slid off. Luckily, she landed back on the swim grid so I reached down over the stern, and pulled her in by the scruff of the neck.

Jodi and Jana were with us for a one week portion of the summer, and that evening, at anchor, the four of us passed the time with a game of Dominoes. I got up after the game was done, to check on the whereabouts of the cat, out on deck I heard that fresh in my mind 'skeeeeeee' sound, after I called her name. I recognized the sound immediately. We knew she'd gone into the water.

Well, she can't walk, but she'll float!

By the time we rushed out on deck and pulled the net out of its resting place at the side of the cabin, Bebe had paddled up the starboard side, around the bow, and down the port side. I ran following her, net in hand, but she swam faster than I could run. She had made an almost full lap around the boat before I could hand the net to Bill, standing back where he could cut her off and dip her out.

Our best guess was that Bebe had jumped into the skiff, that was now drifting close to the boat, jumped back to the rail when she heard me calling, and slid off the rail into the water. She wasn't particularly boat smart yet, but on the plus side, we knew now that she could swim like a fish!

The original fish-boat-cast iron stove was a lesson she only needed to learn once. Usually the stove wasn't on, the weather being warm enough to do without its heat. When we went farther north, after dropping the girls off to return home, the weather grew colder, so it was on almost all day. One afternoon I watched Bebe traverse the length of the counter and stop at the stove's edge. I shouted at her, "NO!" She stopped and looked at me. Again, I commanded, "NO!" very sharply.

Bebe stood frozen at the edge of the stove, one paw raised.

WHAT WRONG WITH ME? I FEEL SO FULFILLED!

I insisted, "NO!" Another second of defiant stares at each other, and then, to my horror she hopped onto that hot stove with both front feet. She bounced off as if she'd been shot, shaking and licking her paws furiously. The pads of one foot were completely blistered. Another lesson learned, the hard way.

Evidently, she hadn't learned enough yet. We were at anchor and tied to a friend's boat in Bergoyne Bay. Ray's boat, although lovely, was still being worked on.

Bebe hopped over the rail to the adjoining boat, and decided to explore. At one point I wondered where she was, and, after some searching, poked my head through the lazarette door, which I discovered open. I found her sitting back behind some pipes, looking like Punk Cat. She was washing a paw.

I managed to reach in and grab her by the scruff, to get her out of there, and get her to stop licking the crap off her feet. She was an abysmal mess, reeking of diesel and covered in rotten oil and/or fuel from head to foot.

I carried her over to our galley, filled the tiny, galley sink with warm soapy water and dunked her in. She stuck all four legs out like an octopus. I couldn't get her to fit in the sink.

There's only one thing more difficult to handle than a wildly squirming, yowling cat ... and that is a *slippery*, wildly squirming, yowling cat. Bill put on a pair of heavy leather work gloves and held her in the sink, but even so, she fought tooth and claw. By the end of it, scratched and bleeding, we knew she could use both tooth and claw.

By the end of the weekend - we had been home for a day and a half by then - we knew by her behaviour, that she was definitely not OK. Monday AM we took her to the vet. She was hydrated for a few hours, given antibiotics ... and a nice long, warm, soapy bath by the vet. I was told that she sat in the bath up to her neck in water, without so much as a squawk. The rotten oil had burned the skin on her belly, her paws and her tushie. Eight hours and $410 later, we brought her home, her fur once again pristine and fluffy. She refused to come out of her travel cage for three days.

Over the next few weeks all the fur on her hind legs, belly, and the bottom side of her tail came out in clumps. She looked like a black and white chicken with whiskers.

It was a nice change from when she first came to us freshly shaved and spayed, looking for all the world like a miniature Holstein cow, with her black and white patches and a hanging pink belly, which looked exactly like an udder!

Rule #36 - *When you get a cat, make sure it's a cat.*

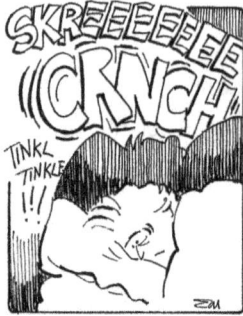

Part VI
BOOBS ARE HIGHLY OVER-RATED

Although the next story involves a very serious subject, I don't think I would have managed very well without a somewhat weird sense of humour. So I shall continue to laugh, as I relate it to you. I hope you laugh too.

THEY CAN'T KILL ME THAT EASILY

In early 2014, we made a long-planned trip in a motorhome, down the west side of the USA, along the Gulf of Mexico to Florida. I dabbled in some SCUBA diving, so included was a 10 day dive trip to St. Maarten, where I celebrated my sixty-seventh birthday underwater. A blown radiator in the middle of the Mojave Desert, a visit to the Daytona 500 race that got rained out halfway through, and the New Orleans Mardi Gras on the way back, pretty much completed the trip.

Once you get past the rubber, they're actually quite tasty!

There was one other little something which I discovered on that trip. I found a very large lump in my breast. I had no intention of missing that dive experience. There was a good chance it would be my last dive vacation. We carried on as if everything was still normal.

As I suspected, when we returned home, I was diagnosed with an aggressive breast cancer. It had already progressed to stage III.

In retrospect, the experience of chemotherapy, radiation, surgery, and all those other delightful things that comprise full treatment, had a profound effect. What doesn't kill you makes you stronger is truth!

▲▲▲▲▲▲▲▲▲▲▲▲▲▲▲▲

There was something else as well, that made everything a little more complex. My mom, at 96 still lived in an assisted living facility.

We all knew that there were a lot of indications that dementia was becoming somewhat problematic. By nature she was a worrier. With the onset of dementia she became Super-worrier.

An example? On the way home from that two month vacation, which included my diving trip, my mother, in spite of knowing I was on the way home, called my sister at least 4 to 5 times a week to cry, "Have you heard from Elly yet?! I just KNOW she's been eaten by a shark! I'm so worried! A shark ate her! I KNOW it!" Poor sister was completely ineffective in dissuading mother of that notion.

When I got home, my answering machine was full of the same messages, all very plaintive, agitated, and making no sense. It was not a good sign. She was convinced I'd been eaten by sharks, until she heard my voice.

On my way to visit mom after we got back, still wondering how she would take my cancer diagnosis, I had a discussion with my sister, telling her it was not a matter of "if", but "when" she would do something inappropriate, and no longer be eligible for assisted living. Mom would have to be moved into full care.

Knowing my mother, I knew she would fight tooth and nail, making life very difficult for everyone.

NancyAnn dropped me off at the facility. I rehearsed how I would tell mom, gently, that I had cancer. I knew some of my cousins were also coming to visit that same afternoon, and I wondered if their presence would help.

She was not in her suite when I opened the door. Her shoes and purse were sitting beside her chair. The walker was gone. Since it was lunchtime, I assumed she'd gone to the early-sitting lunch hour. I walked to the dining room. No mother. I buttonholed one of the staff. No they hadn't seen her ... wait ... oh yes, they saw her sitting in the lobby, waiting for me.

Panic set in when she could not be located anywhere in the building. I began searching the surrounding streets. Still no mother. A short while later, the home got a call from the local hospital. Mom had been picked up from the street by ambulance, and brought in. She had fallen, appeared very confused, but knew enough to tell the admitting staff her name, and the facility where she lived.

I called NancyAnn again, and asked, "Remember the con-versation we had earlier, about 'when', not 'if'? 'When' has arrived!"

When we got to the hospital, mom was still in emergency, in a great deal of pain. She couldn't stand on her feet at all. There was no way I could tell her now, what was going on with me. She had enough to deal with.

It was concluded that she had, in a state of dementia-fuelled thought, gone to the store (she didn't know where it was) shoe-less and purse-less, "to buy some items (which she didn't need) to serve with coffee, for her guests." It spelled the end of

I need some souvenirs to take home. What do you think ..
The beer guy, the bald guy, or the guy in plaid?

her eligibility for the province-subsidized assisted living program, and she would be moved to the first full-care bed available in her area. Her dementia had progressed too far. The facility was simply not geared for it.

Mother went into full-ninja fight mode, but it was a battle she would not win. It was, to say the least, a very difficult time. I never did tell her that I had cancer. With everything else muddying her mind, I could not put that on her as well.

▲▲▲▲▲▲▲▲▲▲▲▲▲▲▲

I'd been referred to the BC Cancer Centre in Victoria, an hour's drive away from us, and an oncologist to oversee my treatment protocol.

After a lengthy consultation, I learned that I would be undergoing chemotherapy for the next 5 months, starting May 26, and done every three weeks after that, for 8 treatments. After that, a mastectomy, radiation, and 13 more chemo treatments. Meanwhile I had a bone scan which turned up clear, thank goodness, and a heart scan in preparation for the administration of a drug which could possibly affect my heart pump. Oh yeah, *that* filled me with reassurance (sarcasm button on). An MRI and CT scans, which also turned up clear, however, did. The oncologist had confirmed that there were a few lymph nodes affected, but the MRI did not indicate a spread to other parts.

On the way down to that first chemo session, it felt surreal. I was filled with trepidation, remembering all the horror stories I'd heard about chemotherapy. I didn't want chemo, but I knew I had to, if I was going to give it my all and have the best chance of survival.

I closed my eyes, and sent a silent and anguished prayer up to the heavens, *"Jesus, help me."* Inexplicably, I felt a very tiny tingle go through me, and a peace that I hadn't had yet. I believe my healing began that day, but I was responsible for my part in the deal.

The day after my first treatment, I spent most of the day in bed feeling like a truck had made contact. No vomiting though. Thank heaven for small mercies, and some very nice drugs. Every day it got just a bit better. By the time a week had passed I felt 50% better, and by the start of the third week, 90%.

The only thing I still had to contend with, was fatigue and digestive problems, along with the feeling I had something permanently stuck in the back of my throat. Maybe that was just my pig-headedness manifesting itself.

I also needed to be very watchful of infection, since my immune system was now severely compromised. Three weeks later, and every three weeks thereafter, I got to do it all over again ... and again .. and again.

Two weeks to the day from the first chemo treatment, I woke up with my scalp feeling as if it had been burned, and I

I don't understand it, but this look seems to be all "the rage" these days!

noticed my hair starting to fall out. I found myself in a hair-shedding competition with my cat. I was winning.

I entertained myself by freaking out my friends and family, yanking clumps of hair off my head and gleefully holding it in front of them.

The Great Shedding didn't happen overnight like in the movies. It started on a Monday, and by Friday, after my shower and shampoo in the morning, the last of my hair was finally off my head and all over the bottom of the bathtub.

I took the clippers and buzzed off the little bit left, and discovered moles I never knew I had! I figured this was the look I started off with in life. My nose just got a little bigger, is all.

Unfortunately the savings on hair products were offset by the expense of scarves and other headgear. I ended up with a perpetually cold head, and a lot of hats. And I'm not even a hat person!

▲▲▲▲▲▲▲▲▲▲▲▲▲▲▲▲

I began shopping for a wig, primarily for the benefit of my mother, who still had no idea I had cancer. I'd gone to visit her often while I still had my hair. She was still in hospital, and stayed for a total of 5 weeks, while they got her walking again.

She was finally discharged, but her return to her assisted living suite was short-lived.

When we got the notice that a bed had been found for her, I had to coordinate her transportation to the new facility, round up help from family to pack up her suite, get it in storage, and deal with all the paperwork to get her signed in to her new digs, all while hiding myself from her, because, at that point I didn't have my wig yet. I felt like a secret agent, in my scarf and hat, skulking around the corner of the care home, until mom was out of sight.

The next time I visited her I wore my new wig. She never noticed that my hair looked a little different. In retrospect, it's probably a good thing I had the habit of changing my hairstyle often.

The care home was an old one, and we were not happy with it. Neither was she. She was very unhappy there amongst "all those crazy people". They'd put her on the dementia floor. I put in a request immediately to have her moved out of her health region on the Maionland to mine on Vancouver Island. Because I had power of attorney for her, and was considered primary caregiver, that could be done. But it took eight months, while the wait list was whittled down to her name, and we watched helplessly as her mental faculties diminished.

▲▲▲▲▲▲▲▲▲▲▲▲▲▲▲

Wearing a wig was not all it's cracked up to be. I felt like I had a critter on my head. My shiny pate, according to most friends, turned out to be my best look, at least that's what everybody told me. Their exact words were, *"You have such a beautifully shaped head!"* Seriously? Did they actually *look?*

After two treatments and another round of endless examinations, my oncologist announced that the tumour and the lymph nodes had shrunk in size. Progress! By the fifth treatment the tumour had shrunk by 50% and the nodes under my arm were undetectable. That bit of good news buoyed me up through the second phase of chemo, which was gruelling.

There were another two drugs involved, and done separately for the first round, to check for any possible allergic reactions. They lasted four hours the first day, and six the second day.

However, the trail of blood in my wake on the chemo room floor after the second day's session, caused a bit of consternation on almost the entire ward. This was due to the IV shunt left in my vein overnight. By the time it came out, there was a sizeable hole in my arm, and I had a wad of gauze and tape on it.

As I was leaving, a lady sitting near the door mentioned to me that she liked my hat. I badly needed to go to the bathroom, (I'd been in the chemo chair for six hours) but I stopped to talk to her for a moment.

Bill was just ahead of me, and he turned around to wait. Two ladies were coming up behind, also in the process of leaving, and I suddenly noticed that all 3 of them were suddenly backing up, staring and pointing at the floor around me, with a look akin to horror. I wondered why, until I looked down myself, and saw large splatters of blood all around me.

While my brain was processing this, with a bit of difficulty, since I still had to pee real bad, I didn't notice that the hole in my arm was bleeding profusely through the wad of gauze, and I waved my dripping arm at all the blood on the floor, babbling like a fool.

"Oooo, blood! blood!", stated I, like Captain Obvious, before I saw that the source was me! The only intelligent comment I could come up with after that was, "I'm leaking!". It served to make a dramatic exit. But I did have my pee first.

When it was determined there would be no side effects from these particular sets of drugs, the treatments were given back to back on the same day, again, every three weeks, taking a total of seven hours.

On one occasion they'd forgotten to mix my "cocktail" before I got there, and by the time that was ready, and the treatment finished, we closed the place down for the night. Near to another appointment, I got busy with something, and totally forgot it. By my reasoning, we were allowed one mistake each, so that pretty much evened the score.

Through it all, my darling Bill was my rock. He accompanied me to every chemo treatment, every oncology appointment, patiently fed me when I didn't feel like eating, held my hand, and never looked sideways when I got bitchy. What a guy!

At the end of the eight rounds of chemo, my oncologist told me that he could no longer detect the tumour. This meant either the thing had been reduced to levels only an ultra-sound, mammogram or MRI could detect, or it was gone totally, not unheard of, according to him. Either way, even though the idea of chemo had scared the crap out of me, and even though it took five

Alright, who's been messing with the chemicals again?

hellish months out of my life, I was so glad I opted for that before surgery.

Strangely, I suddenly developed an unexplainable attachment to my left breast. I found it a bit disconcerting that soon, I would not have this appendage. I'd always said, if I ever got breast cancer, I would have no qualms about having the offending breast removed. But when that abstract became the reality, it wasn't quite so easy to make the same glib proclamation. I had women tell me that breasts were over-rated anyway, who needs 'em! But they were the ones who still had both boobs attached to their chests.

Then I told myself, *Suck it up, you idiot. You want your breast or you want your life?*

Plans for reconstructive surgery became salve for my trepidation. I took comfort in the fact that for the remainder of my wrinkly old age, I would have at least one perky breast, half of every woman's dream!

It wouldn't happen right away. My skin had to be completely healed up from the radiation. I still had that to look forward to after surgery, as well as another thirteen rounds of chemo.

I wondered what it would be like to walk lop-sided for a year or more? Would I list? I wondered if they made a bra that held beer in the empty cup ... with a straw? Maybe I could invent one. Should I apply for a patent? Oh, the questions! What else could I fill it with? Candy? Nah ... Too much sugar ... fattening. My cell-phone? Nah, that thing supposedly grows tumours in unlikely places. Money? I challenge any pick-pocket to try and filch my wallet from that spot. I could smuggle stuff through airport security. No. I'd probably be put on a no-fly list. I still liked the beer idea the best ... with a straw! Bill promised to buy me a one-holer bra for Christmas.

While I walked around half boob-less, I found a pair of soft silicone forms at Wal-Mart, of all places. These things were actually designed to "lift" ladies' boobs, if they felt a little under-endowed. The largest pair were roughly the same size as my one remaining boob, so one of them made a great temporary filler in my empty bra cup.

The only problem was, if I bent over too far, the thing would fall out and plop on the floor, or sidewalk, or wherever I found myself. It was a bit embarrassing, but then, I'd just remind myself, hey, I'm cheering someone's day up with a laugh! I couldn't help but think of ways I might play practical jokes on people with the thing. One scenario played out in my head, where I'd be sitting in a pub or similar venue, and find some guy staring at my boobs (oh yeah, as if) and I'd whip the thing out, shove it under his nose and say, "Ya wanna see my boobs? Here! Take a closer look!" I'll admit it. I'm weird.

My head started showing more growth than just insignificant fuzz, which was very pale in colour with just a few dark ones scattered in. I didn't know if that was an indication of the the colour coming in, and, could I get away with calling it "Platinum Blonde"?

What I missed most was eyebrows. My face was expressionless and somewhat old looking without them. Remember my vanity? It's still intact, even as we speak. People! Listen to me! Appreciate your eyebrows! They do wonders for your face, wonders, I tell you. Nobody ever appreciates eyebrows. And eyelashes … they really do protect your eyes. I can't tell you how many times I had to rinse my eyes with water because some stinging thing got in them, that normally would not have. I'm not talking about shampoo of course. Duh. (Think about that for a minute) Nobody appreciates eyelashes either … until they're no longer there … then you miss 'em!

My skin also took a big hit from all the chemicals pumped into my system all those months. Yikes! I read somewhere that yogurt did wonderful things for your face, so I plastered on some plain Greek yogurt and zenned out for 20 minutes. My reward? Bill laughing at the hairless, white-globbed creature that was his wife, lying on the couch.

It was very strange to see the beginnings of eyebrows and eyelashes as five o'clock shadows on the edge of my eyelids and where my eyebrows should have been. My face was finally returning.

The mastectomy was scheduled for November, 2014, and the dirty deed was done. It might shock people to realize that a mastectomy patient is in and out of hospital in 24 hours. In by 11 am, and out the next day by 11 am. Seriously, they threw me out the next day, with a hose and bag stuck into the side of my chest, no less! I had to drain and measure the run-off (my terminology) every day.

There's another delightful job. I've had many of those. The hose would not be coming out until the drainage measured a minimal amount. It took three weeks to get to that point. Such relief!

The leash finally gone, I felt as free as a bird, sort of. Half of me was still numb, and the nerve pain I developed was excruciating for awhile. I distinctly remember turning a little snarly at that point. It was not pretty.

In December, when we visited my current oncologist for the last time, he gave the best Christmas present I could have asked for. All breast tissue and lymph node biopsies showed no trace of cancer. For all intents and purposes I was cancer-free.

As soon as I had a half-decent amount of hair, about an inch, I felt comfortable visiting my mother, sans wig. She was still on the mainland in her full care facility. It was Christmas, 2014. The after effects from the mastectomy were manageable, although I still couldn't hug anyone too hard.

I was a little nervous, walking up to mom without the wig. At first she looked at me a little sideways. Then she said, "*You look different!*" For a moment I didn't know how to respond. Then, in a sudden fit of inspiration I told her, "*Yeah. I got a haircut, and they cut it a bit too short!*" She bought it. Luckily, I still had the ability to lie to her face, and get away with it.

▲▲▲▲▲▲▲▲▲▲▲▲▲▲▲

2015 rolled around, and radiation, all five minutes of it, involved most of my days, everyday, Monday to Friday for five weeks. The radiation was designed as an extra insurance, to mop up any currently undetectable cancer cells left. Ditto for the coming thirteen rounds of chemo.

Back and forth I travelled on a 100 kilometres round trip between Duncan and Victoria, thanks to a volunteer organization called *Wheels for Wellness* that provides transportation for people to get to clinics and treatments. We may have worn out the highway. They're still filling in the potholes.

Radiation burn is nothing to laugh at. I resembled a cross between a lobster and a bag lady, because the only thing I could tolerate on my body was the biggest, oldest, softest shirt I could find. I felt so attractive. A good friend had given me a large jar of very heavy Glaxal Base™ skin cream, that she instructed me to slather on after every treatment. It would help with mitigating the burn. I hate to think how much worse it would have felt, if I hadn't used it!

Throughout all of this, I still had the pleasure of being hooked up every three weeks to an IV, for those final thirteen rounds of chemotherapy, now being done in our own local hospital. The only bright spot? There were virtually no side effects except for the destruction of my fingernails. With the consistency of croissants, even a good head scratch caused multiple layers of nail to peel back like flaky pastry.

My hair came back my usual dirty blonde, surprisingly with less grey, and a little curly. I don't recommend curling your hair with this method. It didn't last anyway. The curls dropped out after a two inch growth.

In April of 2015, we finally got notification that there was a bed available for mom on Vancouver Island, where I lived. The home was walking distance from my house.

More hurdles stood in our way, with a flu outbreak at her current home. No visitors were allowed in. The move was delayed. Her placement was in jeopardy, in danger of being given to someone else. I had no reassurance that she'd be placed in that same facility later, and I wanted her there. We waited a week, then went anyway - rules be damned, defied the no visitors order, and got her out. Nobody stopped us.

Mom seemed to perk up in the new place, and was more alert, enjoying the visits I could now make every day. We were all there for Mother's Day. By now she was in a wheelchair, no longer able to walk, or stand on her own two feet. Her dementia progressed to the point where she was convinced that she could still walk, and had fits of temper when she found herself strapped into a chair. She was a feisty one, after all. She never believed that she couldn't walk.

Every effort was made to make sure she did not get up to try, because any consequent fall would have had catastrophic results. She'd already fallen 13 times in the past year, never broken anything, tough old broad that she was, but was always badly battered and bruised.

Shortly after Mother's day, mom managed to do just that. Early one morning, she found the clip that tethered her to her bed, (which would set off an alarm, if she did get out) undid it, and got out of bed, intent on going to the bathroom on her own steam. She fell immediately and hard, hitting her head on the edge of the bed. The shock was too much for her body. Six days later she was gone, one month, to the day she moved in. She was 97, the same stubborn, pig-headed and feisty Dutch lady that she started out as.

She'll undoubtedly have a few words for me, when I see her again.

Rule #37 - *Cry when you need to. Laugh when you want to. It might not change anything, but it'll make you feel better.*

WHEN I AM OLD, I SHALL LOOK IN THE MIRROR

My hair looks like last year's bale of hay ..

yikes! Is that grey?

Is that a jowl? ... I'm getting jowls? .. and bags ...

.. here's a zit! Don't tell me I'm getting those again ...

Well, I suppose there's always such a thing as growing old gracefully!

AND I SHALL GO OUT, AND BUY NEW CLOTHES TO HIDE ALL MY BAD PARTS ....

Here's a lovely outfit, that's positively you!

This top is way too big ...

.. and the pants are too tight!

I'm not in the change room! I'm in DENIAL!!

... AND WHEN THAT DOES NOT WORK, THEN I SHALL TAKE TIME FOR MYSELF, TO RUN LIKE THE WIND,

TO MAKE ME STAY YOUNG, AND STRONGER THAN I WAS.... AND WHEN THAT DOES NOT WORK, THEN ..
WHEN I AM OLD, I SHALL TRY HARD EVERY DAY

TO BECOME MY VERY BEST SELF. AND WHEN I AM DONE ...
KNOWING I'LL HAVE TO DO IT AGAIN TOMORROW, AND THE DAY AFTER THAT, OVER AND OVER, FOREVER .....
THEN .. WHEN I AM OLD,
I SHALL SIMPLY SAY, *PISS ON THIS!*
.. AND SLEEP LIKE A BABY.

Today is a new beginning ...

UNHH

Yessir!! PUFF PUFF PUFF PUFF PUFF PUF PUF PU

.. no more couch potato! From now on, the operative word is ENERGETIC!

Z

EPILOGUE

2022

There has been a world-wide pandemic since March of 2020, and people are doing one of two things. Either they're doing what they need to be doing, to keep themselves, and society in general, healthy and safe, or they're not. There are those that have become (my opinion only - don't get your knickers in a knot) quite silly. They've believed misinformation for truth, or spread conspiracy theories and fear-mongered, harassed health care workers and store employees alike, along with anyone else trying to stick to the plan, and refused to wear a mask and/or get the vaccine. I chose the former. I am a rational person after all. I trust the science, the same science, by the way, that was invented by God Himself.

By now, all after-effects from my surgeries have tamped down to a dull roar, and my life had returned to normal, whatever that means. The permanent nerve damage in my chest, arm and abdomen, I now count as "normal". The credit goes to three things. As I explained to my last oncologist, who oversaw the final chemo treatments, *"There's no combination like God and chemotherapy!"*

And the third thing? The ability to have a good laugh at yourself. Often.

As you may have surmised, there is a life after cancer, if you're lucky and/or blessed to survive like I did. My younger sister did not. She died of ovarian cancer on Jan. 12, 2022. I miss her, but I know it won't be forever.

I am still very much cancer-free. In spite of the breast reconstruction surgery going somewhat sideways, and being left with more permanent nerve damage across my abdomen because of it, I'm still finding reasons to laugh! I'm still trusting God for everything beyond my control. Don't get me wrong. I don't have all the answers. But I trust the sources of what I do know.

The work I had going with local papers as an editorial cartoonist dried up due to the changed times. To stay sane during the multiple lock-downs, and revised social norms generated by Covid-19, I developed a cartoon storyline that has taken on a life of it's own - the silver lining in the dark cloud of a dangerous virus spread. It's called "Grampa Was an Alien". There is now a series of books on Amazon. More are being written. The full books list done so far is on the last page of this book.

In the middle of this, I also illustrated Teresa Schapansky's 12 book children's educational series called "Along the Way", showcasing our great country of Canada. That project was finished in the space of six months. Bill always knew where to find me, glued to my drawing table, or behind the computer.

May every one of you find your own silver lining!

The final Rule in Mossman's law: Rule #38
When all else fails, call it 'normal', and move on.

Remember, when you're having a bad day, just stop ... take a deep breath, and reflect on ...

ummmm ...

Would you excuse me, just for a moment? ...
moment . . .

AAAAAAA

Ahem ... as I was saying ....

✂ The RULES ✂

1. If you're going somewhere, assume you'll end up somewhere else.

2. If you have certain expectations, you can expect triple of what you didn't.

3. If the kitchen floor moves, you may not be at home.

4. Rabbits' feet don't work. Lying through your teeth does.

5. When it looks bad, it might be good, maybe not. Ya takes yer chances.

6. If you plan on having an Achilles heel, footwear won't help. Get full-body armour

7. Sanity is good. Paranoia is more fun.

8. You'll find love in strange places. Proceed at your own risk.

9. Common sense is relative.

10. When in doubt, refer to Rule #2

11. Nobody in business sleeps. Sell the bed.

12. If it's cold where it shouldn't be, you can blame us.

13. Beware of friends who tell you about "good things".

14. Never complain about anything. The opposite of what you don't like is just as bad.

15. You really do come back from a vacation looking different.

16. Not all tans turn out the same colour .

17. It takes an amazingly long time for sand to finally exit your ears

18. Not everything you put into an oven produces something edible.

19. Everything fastened, comes loose. Everything.

20. Rule #5 applies, in reverse.

21. Use the terms "cheaper" & "relaxing" together at your peril.

22. If you want a quiet life, never have a cat door.

23. Expectations are over-rated. Closely related to Rule #2

24. Never flush a third time.

25. If it's raining inside, the "open umbrella = bad luck" rule doesn't count.

26. Not everyone can give or take directions. In this case, following your nose works just as well.

27. When in Mexico, stick to Mexicans. The Gringos are crazy.

28. If it's not stuck to your forehead, you won't have it when you need it.

29. Not all gifts contain good things. Open at your own risk.

30. When driving, always have four spares in the trunk.

31. Dead cats do have their purpose.

32. Good deeds never go unpunished.
(Borrowed from somewhere, but it fits)

33. Marry as close to home as possible. You never know if the wedding gods are having a bad day.

34. Open shed doors slowly and carefully. Odds are there's something on the other side, that will scare the crap out of you.

35. Rum fixes everything.

36. When you get a cat, make sure it's a cat.

37. Cry when you need to. Laugh when you want to. It might not change anything, but it'll make you feel better.

38. When all else fails, call it 'normal' and move on.

80CR

BOOKS BY ELLY MOSSMAN

SERIES FOR KIDS

Grampa Was an Alien
a graphic novel series

1 - Grampa's Curious Vacation

2 - Over the Moons!

3 - The Pet Daddy

4 - Caution! Boy Ahead

5 - Comeuppance & Karma are Cousins

6 - My Man Ziggy

7 - Don't Trip Over the Learning Curve

8 - the Moon Shine Affair

9 - Grand Theft Saucer

10 - My Reluctant Hero

11 - the Great Underwear Caper

12 - Who's the Alien Now?

The Klaxan Chronicles
The continuation of *Grampa Was an Alien,* in chapter-book form

Book 1 - The Dragons & Snogger Granx

Book 2 - Joh-Peah's Secret

Book 3 - The Ghosts of Eigril

Book 4 - The Oracle

Book 5 - A Continuum of Elephants

Stories Grampa Told Me
Spaceman

The Kid Next Door

Same, But Different

Boy, Oh Boy

Don't Wanna Be No Hero

SERIES FOR KIDS, continued

Olivia Petunia

The Cow that Barked
The Man in the Moon
The Magic Pebble
The Tick-Tock Clock
The Fairy Tree

The Cat is Bonkers!

Adventure 1 - Home is Not a
Cardboard Box

Adventure 2 - Captain on the
Bridge!

OTHER KID'S BOOKS

Nmp-Chks & Numskuls - *a full-length
graphic novel*

The Ballad of Blue Eagle Bill - *an Epic
poem, in large print*

The Night Before Christmas - illustrated

BOOKS FOR ADULT READERS

Wait, ... WHAT?
*True funny stories (and not-so-true-cartoons) to
tickle your funny bone*
The Baker From Krabbendam
*A biography, The story of one man's struggles in
the Netherlands and emigration to Canada.*
Fish & Chips
Cartoons, depicting the lighter side of fishing

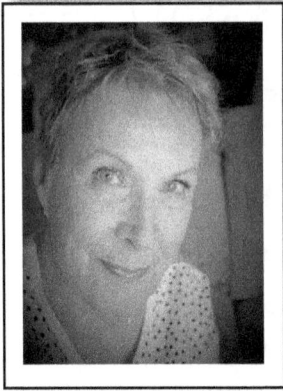

ABOUT THE AUTHOR

Elly Mossman lives in the Cowichan Valley, Vancouver Island, BC, and writes for all age groups, including adults. She is the author/illustrator of numerous kids' book series, including, among others; the graphic novel series, *Grampa Was an Alien.* and *Olivia Petunia.* Other children's work include, *The Ballad of Blue Eagle Bill*, (an illustrated epic children's poem), and the full-length graphic novel, *Nmp-Chks & Numskuls.* Serious oil paintings, graphite and conté drawings, and portraits, both human and animal are also included in her body of work.

She has won four awards in the annual Canadian Community Newspaper Awards for her creative, editorial cartoons, three years consecutively, along with other recognitions throughout her life.
Mossman also illustrates for other author such as Teresa Schapansky, and David Mossman.

Living with her is husband Bill, who on occasion, serves as her inspiration for characters in her books (Nmp-Chks & Numskuls, The Ballad of Blue Eagle Bill). Their cat, Bebe, inspired the series *The Cat is Bonkers!* along with hair covered furniture. Her successor, Mojo will undoubtedly find themselves somewhere in those pages soon.

For more information, please visit:
www.grampawasanalien.com
or contact her directly at kribldor@gmail.com.

www.ingramcontent.com/pod-product-compliance
Lightning Source LLC
LaVergne TN
LVHW051745080426
835511LV00018B/3234